FAST-DRAFT YOUR MEMOIR

Write Your Life Story in 45 Hours

RACHAEL HERRON

ISBN: 978-1-940785-41-7

HGA Publishing

INTRODUCTION

I fell in love with memoir when I was eleven, upon my first expo-
sure. As if memoir were a virus, I caught it hard. It was 1983. At a
garage sale, I bought a book called, *I Should Have Seen It Coming
When the Rabbit Died*, by Teresa Bloomingdale. A slim tome on
Catholic motherhood, I wasn't exactly the target audience, being
neither Catholic nor a mother. I just knew she made me laugh by
telling stories about her children and herself. It was the first true-
to-life story I'd ever read, and while it was no literary masterpiece,
the author had the distinct talent of being able to bring me right
into the story of her laundry, her pregnancy tests, and the way her
many children fought. There was something about the glimpse
behind the curtain that caught me and kept me. She was telling
me stories about *her* life. She wasn't a mountaineer. She hadn't
explored Antarctica or won a war. She was just writing about her
own experience, putting her heart on display, hanging out her
dirty laundry for people to read. I didn't know the author. But I
felt I did, and that, I believe, is the magic of memoir.

I wanted more.

But my parents weren't rich. We shopped at thrift stores and
second-hand bookshops. Sure, there were memoirs by stars and

politicians and big-name athletes, but I found them deadly dull. They read the way they were written—as vehicles to bring attention and adulation to those already attended and adulated.

I wanted to read more real-life stories, and those were harder to find at the flea market. I wanted to read things written by people it felt possible for me to know. Memoirs ghost-written about famous people doing amazing things weren't what I wanted.

Luckily for me, memoir started to pick up in the mid-nineties. I was working in a small independent bookstore when *A Child Called It* by Dave Pelzer came out. A terrible account of a severely abused boy, it was one of the first of its kind: the average person surviving something horrendous. (But, wow, I do not recommend the book. I'm still not quite recovered. Even then, I wanted to read real-life stories, not Jesus-please-kill-me stories.)

The next year, *Angela's Ashes* by Frank McCourt came out to great critical acclaim. Word of mouth made it a bestseller, and when it won the Pulitzer Prize in 1997, even more people got into this "new" trend.

So many of us wanted more of *this*. More of the normal, the real, the heartache, the shame, the everyday, writ gorgeous in language we understood, about the kind of people we already loved. Thomas Larson, in *The Memoir and Memoirist*, says that during this time, the memoir burst forth "sui generis from the castle of autobiography and the wilds of the personal essay."

According to BookScan, which tracks approximately 70 percent of U.S. in-store book sales, "memoirs increased more than 400 percent between 2004 and 2008." [1] And while some say the twenty-year boom of the memoir is winding down, I'd argue the opposite.

Look at YouTube, for example. The reason it's compelling is that we are brought *into* other people's lives. We get a ringside seat, and it's a seat for one. I can sit in my office in Oakland and watch a girl in London teach me how to apply the perfect cat-eye liner from her one-room flat. I get to ogle the posters on her wall.

Her bed is unmade, and that makes me wonder what it means about her that she could post a video with half a million views and climbing and not mind that she hasn't pulled up her bedspread. I get to sit comfortably in my office and judge her for her bed-making skills (though I can guarantee you that at the time you're reading this, my own bed is most definitely unmade).

And, hey, back to me.

You're here either because you heard something about me, or because you accidentally one-clicked your way into purchasing the book and now you're giving it a shot. Yeah, my bed might be unmade, but I know memoir.

A Short History of Rachael Herron's Writing Career

I started trying to write a novel in 1997 when I went to grad school. I wrote three incomplete manuscripts over the next nine years, about 800 pages worth of material. All three of those books are in the proverbial desk drawer and will never come out because I've cast my eyes over them and the writing is *really* bad. It takes everyone time to learn how to write, although it doesn't need to take as long as it took me. If I'd tried to produce more work in those years, I would have learned more, faster. Back then, I didn't know *how* the books were bad—I didn't know enough to be able to articulate their badness. But I couldn't finish them, and that's because I hadn't structured them right (though I didn't know that then).

I despaired, often.

I thought I'd never write a book, even though it was the *one* thing I wanted most in the world.

On Halloween, 2006, my sister Christy and I sat on my back porch, having a glass of wine and hiding from the teenagers prowling for treats. The lights were out in the house, and we were eating Halloween candy right out of the bowl. I'm not proud of that fact, but hey, three anxious dogs who bark at the doorbell, combined with teenagers the size of grown men (no actual small children trick or treat in my neighborhood), do not make for a calm Halloween night.

Christy grabbed a Mounds. She'd always loved coconut. "Hey, have you heard of NaNoWriMo?"

My mouth full of Special Dark chocolate, I said, "Was that a word I should know?"

"National Novel Writing Month. It's this online challenge started by a Bay Area guy. You write fifty-thousand words in a month. In November."

I gasped and almost choked on a Reese's wrapper. "That's so *dumb*. Who would do that?"

"It's supposed to be written fast."

"And badly!"

"Yeah." She beat me to the last 3 Musketeers. "That's the point. You get a lot of not-good writing done so that you can revise it later."

"I think that sounds like a terrible idea." In my head, I said much harsher things: *Oh, HELL, no. I'm a literary writer. I'm trying to write the Great American Novel. That kind of work needs time. Lots of time. Like, years. I'm not a HACK.*

She shrugged and looked up into the eucalyptus that reached over the creek behind our house. We heard and ignored the sound of teenagers screeching like hyenas on the street as we continued to scarf their candy. "Just thought you might like the idea," she said. "Never mind."

Completely predictably, as soon as she left the house, I googled the phrase in the dark, still too scared to turn on the house lights.

NaNoWriMo was a terrible idea.

A real writer wouldn't do something like this, I told myself. A real writer would write all the time, without being forced into writing 1,667 words a day (the number of words it takes a day to "win" NaNoWriMo).

But I wasn't a real writer. I wasn't *writing*. I'd screwed up three books in a row, and I hated all of them. I wrote blog posts and tried to call myself a writer, but even though I had a Master of Fine Arts in creative writing, I felt like a liar.

My hands hovered over the keyboard.

The cursor blinked in the box where I'd enter my email were I crazy enough to take on the challenge. *Sign Up!*

I typed. I confirmed my password.

I was doing this.

NaNoWriMo changed everything for me. Even now, more than a decade later, I'm grateful every day to my sister for suggesting exactly what she knew I needed, and I'm grateful to the founder, Chris Baty, for starting the whole darn thing in the first place.

During that November, I wrote about what I loved instead of what I thought mattered. I'd spent too long trying to write well (whatever *that* meant) and getting stuck, so during NaNo, I just wrote fast. I amused myself. I knew most of it was terrible writing, but I left it. Instead of going back and trying to make it great, I just kept moving forward. Every day I was sure I'd run out of ideas, but every day, the ideas backfilled into the space I'd made for them the day before.

I procrastinated like a true writer, but I still got the words done. On November 20, I blogged, "An alpaca has made a break for it, and I'm about to toss the heroine down a well, and I still can't put a word next to another one. I have, however, tidied four or five separate areas of the house."

I wrote while on vacation in Tahoe. I lay on a motel bed and tried to ignore the squick I felt at touching a Motel 6 bedspread, and I tapped away. I wrote at work in the middle of the night when 911 wasn't ringing, while my coworkers watched TV to stay awake. I took Thanksgiving off from writing and I still somehow managed to finish two days early.

I wrote "The End" for the first time in my life. I was so astonished at the feeling of these tiny but mighty words coming out of the tips of my fingers, I cried.

I opened a dusty can of Sofia Coppola champagne and sat in the sun on the back porch. A November hummingbird zipped by, and the sound of its wings was the sound of my joy. I raised a toast to it, and then to myself. I'd done it. I'd finally finished something. I'd won.

What do you get if you win NaNo, you ask?

On the one hand, you don't get much. You get a celebratory certificate of completion and a very nice email from the staff at the non-profit. Woot.

On the other hand, you claim the biggest gift of your life: *you become someone who finished a whole book.*

That book, after much revision and thirty-two queries, was the book that garnered me my beloved agent, Susanna Einstein, in August 2008. With her help, I did lots more revision, and the book sold in a three-book deal in October 2008. *How to Knit a Love Song* was published in March 2010 (after even more revision!) by HarperCollins, and since then I've published more than twenty books. It still took me a long time to become successful enough to quit my day job. Even with a whole whack of published books, I had to keep my sixty-plus hour a week 911 job until April 2016 (ten years after finally taking myself seriously as a writer and winning NaNoWriMo).

Most of my published books are novels.

But memoir has my heart.

I came to memoir (also known as creative nonfiction, literary nonfiction, and personal essay) from blogging. The same prescient sister had told me about this hot, new trend way back in 2002. In the same older-sister dismissive vein, I'd said something like, "Putting my thoughts up for all to see on a so-called web log? Why would I do that?"

Of course, I started my blog the next day. I originally called it My Glass House since I needed to remember that all who found the blog would be able to see right through the walls.

From the blog I learned one of the most important lessons of writing: people resonated with my work most when I was brutally honest about how I screwed various things up. I wrote about shame and debt. I wrote about guilt and sexuality. When I wrote about how great life was, some people politely said, "Awesome!" When I wrote about how difficult life was in general, and how I was screwing it up in specific, my comment inbox exploded.

So let's make this clear now: no one wants to hear about your perfect life. It's boring.

Similarly, no one wants to hear about how you've been victimized. I hate to say it, but that's just as boring as a perfect life. Even a person who survived a death camp gets tedious if they only talk about how they were hurt.

We want to hear how people failed, how they tried, how they made mistakes, and how they survived in spite of their imperfections.

Your readers want to read how *you* struggled, failed, and got back up.

That's all we want. Show your reader the worst of you, and they'll believe the best. (Caution: the reverse is also true.)

We want to see your broken places and compare them to our own cracks and mended joins.

In 2010, my agent got a request from Chronicle, a press in San Francisco that makes amazingly gorgeous books. You know, those ones that are sold in museum gift shops, the ones you buy people for Christmas? That's Chronicle. They wondered if I had a knitting pattern book they could buy. (I'm a capital-K Knitter and have had yarn either in my hands or on my person since the age of five.)

I didn't have a book of patterns in me, though. I don't write patterns often, and when I do, they're riddled with errors. You're just as likely to get a macramé elephant as you are a pair of mittens if you use one of my patterns.

I do, however, often write *about* knitting, so we offered Chronicle a collection of essays. The memoir's theme was "my life as seen through the sweaters I was making at the time." Don't laugh —knitting has seen me through both the best and the worst of times. I wrote my way through my memories by visualizing what I held in my hands and what was going on around me while I knitted.

My editor at Chronicle bought the book on proposal, and then, in an eminently sensible move, decided that since she'd never edited memoir, they would hire an out-of-house editor to work with me. They hired Jennifer Traig, who was—completely coincidentally—one of my favorite memoirists. I'd fallen hard for her *Devil in the Details,* a memoir about scrupulosity (religious OCD).

And here's what Jennifer taught me: even though I knew I had to show myself in an honest light, I still felt the natural human response to paint myself a *little* better than I was. I wrote about the funny mistakes I made, but I glossed over my broken bits. I mentioned them and then veered away. "Maybe I drank too much that night, but...." Or, "When we broke up, I knew some of it was my fault but..."

No matter what essay I sent her, Jennifer called me out. She'd circle the place I'd spackled over hoping no one would see the hole. She'd write: *This is painful and raw, so it's the place you need to focus on. Throw the rest out. Go deeper into this. Don't back down.*

It was pretty irritating.

But it worked. The essays got deeper. I walked into shame. I smeared it all over myself and stood up in public.

And instead of dying of it? I was freed by it.

Shame researcher Brené Brown says that the one thing that shame can't survive is empathy. When we name our shame, when we shine the spotlight on it and really examine it, we hear from others: *I've been there, too. That must have been hard for you. I get it. I was ashamed of that, too.*

And like that, the shame is gone. It's not eased—it's *gone*.

Think for a moment about how that might change you.

What other credentials should I list before we plunge into doing this together?

Well, I've got that Master of Fine Arts degree I mentioned. [2] I completed grad school in 1999 at Mills College in Oakland and then proceeded to spend seven years writing a whole mess of useless words before getting my act together with NaNoWriMo.

I now teach creative writing in the extension programs at Stanford and Berkeley, something I still can't believe they let me do. I always knew that the only classes I'd ever want to teach were the actual *creation* courses, the ones in which students were actively writing. I didn't want to teach freshman comp to future bankers and lawyers. I had no desire to expound upon gerunds and dangling participles to students who only wanted to paint. So the fact that by getting my masters and then publishing a lot of books I got to skip to the head of the line to teach the super-fun courses is something I never take for granted.

And my absolute favorite class is the one I teach during fall semesters at Stanford: *Fast-Draft Your Way to a Complete Memoir.* Sound familiar? Yes, my intelligent friend, you're right! You're getting everything I know by buying this book, and you didn't even have to spend $650! There's literally nothing I love more than helping writers get their life stories on the page. Their stories are uniquely theirs.

That goes for you, too.

No one can tell your story but you.

You can learn how to do it.

We'll move fast so you can get a draft done quickly, a draft you can revise and make into exactly what you want it to be. We'll learn how to get the work done, and what to do with the book when you've finished it.

You'll do the work, and I'll be honest with you—it's not easy. But with the right tools, it's completely doable. You *can* do this.

I'll show you how.

Chapter Two

WHAT IS MEMOIR, ANYWAY?

"Memoir" is a fancy word for a story about yourself.

It sounds highfaluting, doesn't it? Well, yes, it's French. *I'm writing a MEMwah.* Now, I'm the kind of person who doesn't speak any French at all, so I agree, memoir does sound showy, especially when posted next to the very dry word *autobiography*.

Want to know the difference between memoir and autobiography? It's simple.

Autobiography is the story of your life. Technically, you should only be able to have one of these. (This rule has been pushed around a little bit, but we won't worry about it. People with two autobiographies are greedy, and we don't want them at our hot tub party because they don't respect the definitions of things and would probably break a glass on the deck).

Autobiography is written by you, at or near the end of what you think your best years might be. If you're a hundred and three and reading this book: number one, congratulations! I hope you're one of those drank-a-fifth-of-whiskey-and-smoked-yourself-into-old-age people. Number two, I hope to convince even you, my leathery friend, that you'll still be better served by writing a memoir.

An autobiography is a chronological story of where you were born, how you grew up, how you changed, and where you landed at the end. As Quentin Crisp said, "Autobiography is an obituary in serial form with the last installment missing."

And this can be a very fine story. It's possible that you are a Very Important Person and that people will be fascinated to learn that your mother used safety pins on your cloth diapers. It's possible that the more you tell us about every single class you took at Harvard, the more interested we will be.

But let's think about this objectively.

Imagine you're attending the wedding of a friend. For some reason, you've been placed at the table with all the other people who came alone, and you don't know any of them. On your left is a man. On your right is a woman.

You say, "Hello. I'm an introvert. Being alone at a party is my very special version of hell. Can you please tell me about yourselves to make me feel less like slitting my wrists on the ice sculpture of the lovely couple swing dancing?"

The man says, "Well, yes. I was born on a dark, rainy day in Kansas. My first memory is of the dry kibble in the cat food bowl. I assume that's because I was crawling on the kitchen floor. The next thing I remember is pulling myself to standing at the back of the couch."

You start to blink wildly. Maybe if you do it hard enough, the woman on your right will notice your distress and step in to help.

And she does! She waits politely until the man has to draw a deep breath to continue his soliloquy on how lovely his second day of kindergarten was, and then she says, "When I was twenty, I hopped on a cargo ship to Mallorca. It took five months to get there, and when I arrived, I was broken-hearted, penniless, and pregnant."

Toward which person are you going to shift your wine glass?

Sorry, guy, I want to hear *her* story about the ne'er-do-well who knocked her up and left her in a foreign land.

That's a story.
It's not the story of a life.
It's a *piece* of it.

A memoir is:

- The story of a specific slice of *time* in one's life or
- The story of (or stories on) a specific *theme* in one's life.

The Theme-Based Memoir

My first memoir is called *A Life in Stitches* (Chronicle, 2011). As I said before, the book is collected essays about what was happening in my life as seen through the sweaters I was knitting at the time. This is a *thematically-organized memoir*. I was able to jump around in time because each chapter tied back in to my knitting life.

The idea came to me after my agent asked me, "Well, if not a pattern book, what could we give them?" I was in my home office, which is also the storage room for my yarn and sweaters. I shifted a cat off my lap and swung around in my knock-off Herman Miller chair. I eyeballed the walls of the office, searching for inspiration.

My gaze landed on the middle bookcase, which was full, not of books (those are elsewhere in the room), but of sweaters.

Piles of sweaters. Gobs of them, along with myriad scarves and shawls and hats, stacked high in the ubiquitous Ikea Billy bookcase. Faced with a storage crisis of growing proportions, I'd taken the sweaters out of the closet and put them where I could see them and remember to wear them.

I realized they told a story.

My story.

I started at the top, looking at the green and white sweater I'd made when my mother was dying. As I'd knitted it at her bedside —a direct copy of a sweater she'd comissioned for herself in Norway in the 1960s—I'd recreated the arms that had held me as a child.

The sweater below that was the one I'd made when I was secretly engaged to my now-wife. We'd only been together for six months, and we knew everyone would laugh and make U-Haul jokes if we said we were getting married, so we kept it a secret for a few months longer. But I wore that sweater all the time, and every time I looked down at the hearts encircling the left wrist, I felt warmed even though I'd made it out of cheap acrylic. *shudders*

My sweaters, seen together, told a story about me. Some of the chapters in the finished collection include: trying (and failing) to knit my wedding dress, the boyfriend-curse sweater, and the blanket I made when I was at my poorest while living in a hovel that shouldn't have housed pigeons. The sweaters, written about individually, gave a backdrop for my chapters. They were the background music.

Honestly, it almost doesn't matter *what* framing device you use in telling your story, as long as there is one. In *To Show and To Tell*, Philip Lopate says about his essay collection on the New York waterfront: "A confession: I was never obsessed with the waterfront. It offered a pretext and a structure for me to follow out my interests in a dozen different directions. This formula of curiosity-driven research plus personal voice is one of the most prevalent modes in today's successful nonfiction, from Rebecca Solnit to Philip Gourevitch to Jonathan Raban, from travel writing to nature writing to family chronicles to political investigations. Not obsession but curiosity." [3]

Lopate used the waterfront to organize his thoughts. I used

sweaters. Mary Karr uses her history of substance abuse in her book *Lit*.

In a theme-based memoir, you can use just about anything. Have you been obsessed with pens your whole life? Write an essay about each one—what it meant to you, what you wrote with it. Or are you a fan of a particular sports team? Talk about what the games have meant to you over the years. You can jump around in time; you can leap from being married to being a kid and back to becoming a grandmother.

One thing about the theme-based memoir, though: it's harder to create a narrative arc in a book that turns out to be a collection of essays. (We'll talk about narrative arc soon.) An overall arc should exist in your collection, even though the essays might stand alone. It requires some extra tweaking and some judicious pruning. A theme-based memoir, because of this, has an inherent danger built into it: your reader can walk away at any time, and she might. If each essay in the book stands on its own merit—if each one is a tiny, perfect story—then except for your excellent writing abilities, you have nothing else with which to draw the reader along. At the close of a strong personal essay, the reader will sigh with satisfaction. There isn't any mystery left. There are no cliff-hangers in this format. With luck and good writing, your reader will turn the page because she can't wait to read what you say next (excellent examples include the memoirs by Roxane Gay, Samantha Irby, and Jenny Lawson, to name just a few). But the risk of your reader wandering away to another book is real and present since you have little to no suspense dragging her along behind you.

The Time-Based Memoir

A memoir written about a particular moment in time means that you, as the writer, can lead your reader through that time. There's a clear-cut beginning, a middle, and an end, not only in your writing but also inherent to the span of your narrative.

Some examples include:

Cheryl Strayed's *Wild*: I know you read it. We *all* read it, and boy, is it worth reading. The perfect example of the time-based memoir, it's the story of a trip with a literal starting point and stopping point (the Pacific Crest Trail). It also includes Strayed's personal journal—the interior exploration that she made while she was toting that backpack the size of a small college student.

Jeannette Walls's *The Glass Castle*: This is the story of a girl's coming of age in a household of chaos, framed by her non-chaotic present. It's so iconic and brilliantly written that if you haven't read this one, just buy it already.

Elizabeth Gilbert's *Eat Pray Love*: I don't care if you love or hate this book, it'll make an impression on you, and that's half the battle, folks. Give me a one-star or a five-star rating; as writers we want to inspire strong emotion, even if that emotion is negative. The book is perfectly balanced—a trip to three different countries, with Pray/India being sandwiched right there in the middle, a perfect Act Two. It's hard to *not* finish this book (though plenty of people report being able to).

Time-based memoirs are journeys through time. They're frequently the kind of book new memoirists want to write. My classes are chock-full of students bursting at the seams to tell their Big Story.

You may be one of these people.

You may want to write about:

- The time you sailed to Japan with your brother.

- The twelve years of abuse you received from your birth mother.
- The year you spent in Iraq.
- The six months you took care of your father as he died of tuberculosis.
- The five years you spent battling breast cancer.

Oh, my students say as I tell them that writing this kind of time-based memoir is a common desire. *Does that make me boring? Am I just another person with a recovery memoir?*

Heck, no! Having an idea of what you want to write about is *great.* Having a single story makes things so much easier for you.

The students who have the hardest time with memoir, honestly, are those who have had *too* interesting a life. They come in with the time they ran away from abuse, the time they married a polygamist, and the time they helped their kid kicks drugs, and then they have to choose. *That's* hard.

Wait, my students say. *I have to choose? Why can't I just write a memoir about my whole life?*

Well, that's autobiography. And trust me when I say—again—that no one wants to read the story of your whole life, not even your sweet, forbearing mother who thinks everything you do is fascinating. Please. The most fascinating person on the planet is still regularly boring. (Except for Beyoncé. I bet she's actually rarely boring.) But it's not so bad—you'll choose a book to write (much more on this in the following chapters), and when you finish the first memoir, you can feel free to write the next.

Because that's the magic of memoir. A twenty-year-old can write a good one, just as a seventy-year-old can. We can all have multiple memoirs, with different themes and time frames.

Writing memoir is addictive. It's hard to stop at just one.

Exercise:

We're going to dive more deeply into what kinds of memoir exist, but ask your gut right now—which direction are you leaning? Will you write about a slice of time or about a certain theme?

Chapter Three

REASONS NOT TO WRITE MEMOIR

You bought this book because you'd like to know how to write your memoir. Perhaps you even want to write it quickly. Fabulous.

Welcome aboard the ship of memoir! But before you make yourself *too* comfortable on board, before you claim your sleeping berth and find out where the captain keeps the cognac, I want to talk to you about the reasons you might want to disembark before the last whistle blows.

The Anger Memoir

Memoir isn't for you if you're holding a grudge. I can't tell you how many people I've met through my classes who want to write the "punishment" book. Someone was terrible to them. They were victimized. They were done wrong. With this memoir, they'll set the record straight. It's the equivalent of swinging through the saloon doors with a chip on your shoulder and a gun in your hand. It doesn't end well for anybody.

But I was REALLY done wrong. I barely survived. And I hate the people who hurt me.

I bet that's absolutely true, and seriously, I'm so sorry that happened to you. I wish it hadn't.

But you've got problems in memoirlandia. First, the reader won't believe you. Second, it's *annoying.*

You won't keep a reader reading (your biggest job as a writer) if you're busy being angry at someone else. When people whine about how sorely they were treated, we wonder what they did to deserve it. Isn't that awful? We *shouldn't* be that way. It's a moral failing. But it's human nature.

And please let me be clear: horrible things happen to good people, things that are worthy of true, deep anger. These things can and should be written about.

But you cannot punish others with your writing. You can't get even by writing a memoir. You won't be able to reap revenge. Trust me, the person you want most to read your writing, the one you want to stick it to, won't read it (they're often dead), and even if they did read it, they wouldn't change or ever see your side of it.

You can only help heal yourself with your writing. Please feel free to do that. Honestly, paying for good therapy will help you way more than struggling to write an anger memoir (and it'll be cheaper in the long run if you tot up what your time is worth). As Mary Karr says in *The Art of Memoir,* "Your psychic health should matter more than your literary production." [4]

The I'm So Awesome Memoir

Are you? Are you so awesome that everyone will want to read every bit of your awesome life?

Nah, you're not. No one is that great, and no one should try to be, *especially* not on the page.

To be brutally honest, looking fantastic in memoir is an idea that usually comes to me from straight white male doctors and ex-military men of a certain age. I bet if you're not one of those, you're not in much danger of wanting to write this kind of memoir.

If you do, however, want to write about how well you did in battle, or how many lives you've saved over the years with your research and your bare hands, pull back a moment and think about it from another angle.

Perfect people aren't interesting.

Luckily, you're not perfect! Even if everyone else in the world thinks you are, *you* know you're not, and that right there is where you want to pan for gold. We'd love to see your awesomeness on display as long as you can also show us your flaws. For every great story about how you saved the day, we'll need at least five embarrassing stories that show you broken in the same way your reader is. Empathy springs from sharing shameful secrets, and your reader will love you for displaying the real you to her.

The I'm So Sad Memoir

This one comes in many flavors. The memoir might be about divorce, loss of a child, loss of health, or loss of self.

Before you pledge to write this, do a gut check. Can you talk to the barista at Peet's about this particular sadness without bursting into loud, public tears? When you think about writing it, do you give yourself a grief migraine? Do panic attacks come on the heels of telling your best friend about the idea?

You're too close to it, my friend. You won't be able to write about this grief until you can step back and watch yourself, in both the past and present tense.

Our job as memoirists is to be able to not only report what

happened, but what it meant. It's a balance of showing *and* telling. If your heart is so fragile that it requires constant care (and after great grief, it will), you're simply not in the place you need to be to write this now. Take heart, though. You will be. Eventually. We do heal from grief, though we live our lives with that limp of the soul forever after. In his memoir *Levels of Life*, Julian Barnes writes about the death of his wife: "Nature is so exact, it hurts exactly as much as it is worth, so in a way one relishes the pain, I think. If it didn't matter, it wouldn't matter." [5] If you're lost in a vortex of grief, that's because what you loved was worthy. When the sea of tears inside you becomes a creek and then a summer trickle, you'll be ready to write your grief memoir. But not until you can talk about the idea without (always) crying. Some crying is okay. It's expected. But be honest with yourself. Trust your gut as to whether you're in the right place to be objective about your journey.

The I Have a Terrible Memory Memoir

This is a trick! I put it in here because you don't have to worry about this.

If you have a terrible memory, *you can still write a great memoir.*

Memories are formed in both the amygdala and the hippocampal cortex. They make up two independent memory systems, but they act together when emotion meets memory. [6]

Even more simply stated, when you experience strong emotion, memories are strongly formed and are easier to recall later. These heightened-intensity memories tend to be more solid, real, and granular. This is why, after a car crash, we remember the song that was on the radio, the way the dashboard looked when it cracked, and exactly what the other car sounded like as its bumper crumpled. As emotion goes up, so does the brain's ability to write memories to long-term storage.

So, you may not remember a single thing about the ages six to fourteen except for when your mother said she couldn't forgive you for your brother's broken arm. You might not even remember how he broke it, but you remember the look on your mother's face as she told you weren't her favorite and never had been. That moment is crystalline because it went along with great emotional pain.

If you have a few of these? You can find more. And if you don't remember things perfectly, that's okay. We have things we can do about that. But take heart, my forgetful Dory. You can still write your memoir.

Chapter Four

FAMILY: CAN'T LIVE WITH 'EM, CAN'T WRITE ABOUT 'EM

Oh, family. Relatives are not only the reason for the season, but they're the reason we start drinking once the first holiday lights are up, am I right?

Okay, *you* might be one of those charmed people who come from a perfect home. Mom is a doctor and gardener and makes her own bread when she's not counseling young single mothers, and Dad is a lawyer and musician who does pro-bono work for the homeless. If everything in your life has been great—well, I'm pretty damn sure you wouldn't want to write a memoir if that were true. If you *do* want to write one, you've probably had some shit go down and you want to tell us about it, which is why you picked up this book.

So, I'm going to just assume that none of you come from perfect homes.

And along with that comes the assumption that you'd like to write about your family. Maybe it's not the entire thrust of your memoir (if you're writing about your year experimenting with ayahuasca in the Amazon, you might be able to skip over Mom's addiction to QVC), but the truth is, you came from somewhere.

The somewhere you came from and the people who were there have helped shape you into who you are now.

And you should probably write about them at some point if you want to be honest with your reader, *which you do.*

Readers are incredibly intelligent. The moment you gloss over something because it feels uncomfortable, they'll notice. I guarantee it. A reader who thinks you're covering something up will have zero motivation to get to know you better. There are a million great things to read out there—she'll touch the Home button on her Kindle and open something else, leaving you forever.

You have to be honest with your intelligent reader, and you have to keep her engaged.

At the same time, you don't want to hurt Aunt Christina in a way that will be make her as angry as she got when Uncle Bob cheated on her and she filled his Corvette with the fireworks he'd bought illegally in Montana, setting them all off and burning down not only car but the town's gazebo in the process. You love Aunt Christina. And you like your car and would like it not to burst into flames. Still, you *really* want to write about the time she shamed you in front of your third-grade class by stage-whispering that you were "a tiny freak of nature" in a voice that carried to the next county.

In my classes, the worry about how to handle family is the biggest one of all.

- "If I write about what my mother was really like, she'll disinherit me and my kids."
- "If I write about my sister, she'll know how I really feel about her, and I can't bear for her to know."
- "If I write about my husband, he'll leave me."

- "If I write about my kid, I'll scar him forever."

These are huge stakes. I'm not going to pretend they're not.

And you might not be wrong. I'd love to tell you that you are —that if you write about the night your father hurt you, the family reunion will be the same. But it might not be.

Anne Lamott famously said, "You own everything that happened to you. Tell your stories. If people wanted you to write warmly about them, they should have behaved better." [7] This has been taken by some new memoirists to mean they should write all of it, screw everyone's feelings.

But most don't know Lamott also said, "I know I'm not going to publish anything that anyone I'm close to would be hurt by or would hate. And I know how much I'll end up taking out. Telling the truth in memoir isn't telling *all* the truths. It's not spewing. Anything I'm writing will be completely crafted and edited before it's published." [8]

Some Things to Keep in Mind

There's no way this book of yours is ever, *ever* going to be read by anyone without you planning extensively for that day. It will not accidentally be sold to an editor and jump onto the bookshelves of the Safeway around the corner to be picked up by your aunt who was just there looking for some Camels and the new *People* magazine. *If* you choose to publish this book, you'll have months —if not longer—to prepare how you'd like to present this information to those who might read it.

Every memoirist handles the problem of family differently,

and I don't have the best answer for you. This is something you'll have to figure out, but the key is: *you figure this out later.*

Right now?

Right now, you write as if every single person involved were dead.

Morbid, right? Did you just suck in your breath a little bit? Did it hurt to think about? Good, you're human.

But do it anyway.

Write as if you're ninety-seven years old. All the people you've ever loved are gone, and you're in a bright and happy nursing home where you're kept in peanut butter and nightly ping-pong. Life is good, and you're now going over the events that filled your active years.

Write about what your father did without thinking how it might affect him (or anyone who knew him). They're *all* dead, remember. You get to be completely, bone-achingly honest. Write about the time your mother hurt you to the core. Tell your story honestly about what it was like to know your brother was being molested and you had no idea what to do about it.

These things are *yours.*

You were there.

You own them.

When questioned at a reading on writing about his brother's affair with a woman twenty-two years his senior, renowned memoirist Andre Dubus III said, "What happened on my brother's side of the wall was his story. What I heard on my side of the wall was mine." [9]

Even if you were not the done-to abused party, you own the remnant traces of abuse that washed up and splashed your feet. What you heard, saw, wondered, *you* get to write all about it.

You get to conjecture.

You get to be wrong about those conjectures.

And you *should* write all of this down, with the full knowledge that *no one* will see a word of it until you figure out how much you want to share. It's safe to do so.

This is how you write it: by telling yourself they're dead. No one will ever see your words. It's a bit of twisted irony, but you lie to yourself in order to be able to tell the ultimate truth, to put the deepest parts of your heart on the page.

Then, you come up for air when the book is done. After the book is complete, and after you've revised it once or twice with the help of a good editor who is not related to you (more on this later), only *then* do you start to decide how to handle the truths you are going to put out into the world.

Different memoirists have different tactics for this.

First, I personally always make *myself* the most deeply flawed character. I center on this. I do it because it's true and easy—I'm terribly flawed, and I don't mind sharing the many ways I am. I don't write memoir to get even—I write it to find out who I am.

Second, I show nothing to anyone until it's done, done, and *done*. It has to be pretty near perfect—if you're taking a risk by showing someone your work, make sure they can only complain about the content, not the writing itself.

Third, I go through the manuscript and pick out the parts that are about people I care about most. They don't get to read the whole book—oh, no. But they get to read the parts that are specifically about them. I don't use pseudonyms while I'm working because I'm a bear of very little brain and if I start calling my sister Bethany something like Agnes, I will get confused.

I have decided—this is *my* decision, no one else's—that I will not publish anything about my sisters or my wife that they do not want me to. They get ultimate veto power. My relationship with them is strong and deep, and my love for them is vast. I don't want any part of my ego punching them in the face just to tell a good story.

So I go through and highlight the parts that are about my sisters or my wife. Then I give them those parts.

One of my sisters is very private. She nixed a few lines in *A Life in Stitches,* and while I wish I'd been able to keep it as written, I edited to her wishes. They were only very small changes, but had they been larger, I would have also acceded to her request, whatever it was. My other sister isn't as private and usually lets me keep what I write as written. My wife just shrugs and tries not to think too much about the fact that I use her regularly for fodder. But she *could* veto anything about her. She knows that.

I honor my relationships this way. This is my choice.

However, I don't do the same thing with friends or acquaintances. You have more of them than you have family members, and this makes them easier to disguise if necessary.

Let me explain: when my friends pop up in my nonfiction, I give them a bit of power in revision because I love them, but I retain ultimate control (as opposed to giving my sisters and wife all the control by choice). With friends, whatever it is that I'm writing stands. I make those decisions. But I'll send my friend the piece and say, "Would you like me to use your real name in this, or would you like me to disguise you and use a pseudonym?"

If Sophie, for example, doesn't want to be identified as the person who Ambien-tripped me with in a hotel, she gets to say, "No, thanks. Make me someone else." And I'll change her name to Ingrid and give her a different job and a different haircut or age, and there—Sophie's now out of the book and Ingrid is in. Sophie will know who she is. No one else will. (Sophie approved this message.)

For people like exes, or folks who aren't in your life anymore, do yourself a favor. Disguise them well. You don't want a lawsuit. Make the guy who lived in Mississippi live in Montana. Change his name and eye color, so you have deniability.

But isn't this lying?

Oh, we have a whole chapter on truth coming up! Just wait!

This cloaking is almost impossible to do with relatives. If you've only got one uncle, your family will know which one you're referring to. Having only one mother or father makes it harder for you, and I'm sorry about that.

There are several different ways to handle how you present your *finished* work to family. (Again, no showing of drafts. Ever.)

1. It's done!

You can present your book to people as a fait accompli. *Here you go, Sister and Brother.* If you do this, please walk yourself through all the possible ramifications. Mary Karr worried her mother would hate would her book, *Lit*, but instead, her mother embraced the stories. "In my hometown, the seamier facts had been common knowledge anyway, but something about having all the bad news out in open air freed us even more. Call it aversion therapy: we seemed collectively to get over Mother's half-century-plus lies about who she was. When she arranged a book signing at our local library, over five hundred people showed—including old beaus, far-flung cousins, and my first-grade teacher." [10]

If you go this fait-accompli route, though, you need to have some answers about what you'll do if Mom or Dad hates your book and disowns you. You might be okay with that. Only you can answer that.

2. Edit It For Them

You can edit it to their specifications, even if it breaks your vision of the book (this is what I do with my few chosen family members—the rest can lump it). Can you make peace with the possible breaking/changing of your book? And importantly, if you lift out or change those parts, are you still telling the truth? (It's absolutely possible and acceptable to tell the truth in a different way. It's *not* okay to lie, which families are often professional at doing.)

3. Just Forget It

You can resign the book, as is, to the desk drawer, where no one will read it. It's possible that simply writing it set you free in the way you were hoping for.

Let's face it, all of these options are less than ideal.

You might end up hurting people.

You might end up hurting people you don't even plan to hurt. I wrote a piece once about a friend. It was truthful and made her look good while making me look like someone who had some crap to work out. All this was true.

But a different friend thought I was writing about *her*. I wasn't, but I couldn't prove it. There is no way to predict how the people around you will react to memoir, ever (or fiction, for that matter). The people you think will be mad will be tickled, and the ones you didn't write about will either be offended or imagine their way into the book. Knowing this beforehand is helpful.

Also helpful in some cases is planting the seeds of what you're doing in the minds of those you worry about. One of my students was concerned about how her father would react to her writing about him, so without letting him see her pages, she recruited him for help in research. He threw himself into the project, and because he felt that he was helping her, he ended up as proud of the whole thing as if he'd written it himself (even the parts that were about him).

No one knows your loved ones better than you do.

If you love them, take care of them.

But tell the truth.

And what the hell is *that?* We talk about truth in the next chapter.

Exercise:

The Safety Circle

Draw a circle on a piece of paper. (Yes, this one has to be done on paper. You might think you know how this will go if you play it out in your mind, but I guarantee you'll be surprised by what happens when you do this by hand.)

- Inside the circle, put the names of the people you'd trust to read parts of your memoir. They're the ones who won't care what you say, who will cheer you on, who will believe in you one hundred percent (no less!) no matter *what* truths you tell.
- Outside the circle, put the names of the people you'd like to protect your manuscript from while it's in the early stages, while it's learning how to breathe.

My students are always surprised by where people fall. When I did this exercise for the first time, I included my boss at the time in the circle, something that shocked me. We weren't really friends outside the job. We didn't even hang out together, yet I trusted her completely. And my boyfriend, the man I told everything to, was outside of it, which made me feel ashamed. But I knew it was right.

Okay, done? Got the names in the right places without feeling too much guilt?

ESSENTIALLY IMPORTANT: Don't show any part of your memoir to *anyone*.

No one.

Show no part of your memoir to *anyone,* no matter *where* they fall in the circle. Keep this up for the first twelve weeks of working on this project, at least. And under pain of death, never *ever* show anything you write to anyone who's outside the circle of safety until you're getting ready to decide how to publish the book.

Why?

If you show a piece to your husband (even if he's inside the safety circle) and he says, "Oh, I liked it a lot!" you'll still find something defeating about the way he says it.

"You only liked it?"

"No, I loved it!"

"What did you love?"

"All of it!"

"You couldn't have loved all of it. Name me what you really loved."

"That description of your mother. Spot on. Loved it."

"So you hated the rest. That's what you're saying to me?"

And that's to someone inside the circle. If you show a piece that you think is *perfect* to someone outside the safety circle? You might as well kiss the book goodbye forever. I know. You think you can handle this criticism, but you can't. No one can, not when it's memoir.

Unless you're a practiced writer who regularly puts out work and hears criticism all the time, be wary of showing anything to anyone (unless you're in a class of like-minded memoir writers—they get it, and they're strangers, so they're much safer).

And even if you're a professional novelist, please know that writing memoir is different in one big way.

In fiction, if someone mocks something or hates something else, it can hurt, but we can hide behind the fact that it's not true (even though fiction is often incredibly true, even when it's all made up). We get to put up the "I made it all up!" defense. *Yes, my character is an addict, but I'm just imagining it all! Yes, she's mean to her kids, but that's not me!* We have plausible deniability, and we use it.

But in memoir, we go into the deepest parts of ourselves, and we lift them up into the light. We display our broken bits. We show ourselves, naked and flawed.

When someone laughs, or just doesn't get it, it can be devastating. Not only is your writing being criticized (a spear in the side), our very *selves* are being rejected (a beheading).

If you show anything to someone too early, you might not want to go back to it. And I deeply, desperately want you to go on with your work.

Important: If you feel your writing *could* be read by someone while you're writing it—if you have a nosy teenager or spouse, or even just a bored one—**password protect your work right now.** No joke. Do it this instant. You might think you'd be fine if they read your work in progress, but trust me, you won't be, and worse, if you have to defend your writing while it's still barely blushing green, unfurling its careful tips to the warm sunlight, you won't be able to face going back to it. Password protect the file, if not your whole computer.

Chapter Five

TRUTH AND MEMORY

After worrying about family and loved ones, this is the second-most popular item to talk about in every memoir class I've ever taught.

What *is* truth? And how can we trust anything when our memories are fallible?

These are *huge* questions, and while all memoirists have to grapple with them individually, I'm going to tell you my rules.

I want the memoirs I write and read to be true, or as true as the author can make it. This is important to me. If I find out later that she might have stretched truths really creatively or made up parts of her book out of whole cloth, I won't trust anything she says.

You've heard the stories of memoirists who just straight-up lied in their memoirs. Remember James Frey's *Million Little Pieces*, and how Oprah chewed him out on stage? Every time I'm having a bad day, I'm grateful that Oprah has never done that to me. Remember Nobel-prize nominated Greg Mortenson fabricating details of his charity trips?

Not interested. I read memoir for truth.

But within that quest, I'm a savvy reader, as most memoir-readers are. I know that most people don't have a photographic memory (and even people who do have eidetic memories can still experience their memories changing over time). I know that memoirists can't recall *exactly* what their third-grade teacher said, even though the scene and dialogue they write seems to be perfect, down to the details of how the spit collected in the corner of the teacher's mouth as he shouted, "Sit your ass down, or I'll sit you down with the back of my hand."

When I read this, I trust the author remembers this scene. She's not just making it up out of thin air. I also trust her to nail what was said pretty close to the way it actually was uttered. But do I need her to have a photographic memory and prove it to me? No way.

I'll even trust writers who admit their memories aren't that great.

In fact, someone admitting this to me means I'll trust them *more* since they're aware of the fallibility of memory. There's nothing worse than the person who pipes up, yelling that they remember everything exactly the way it happened.

The truth is: no one's memory is infallible.

Even more upsetting to learn is this:
Our memories are changing all the time.

Studies show that each time we take a memory out to admire it, we're changing it just a little. *Every time.*

I'll wait while you collect yourself. No one loves learning this.

Daniela Schiller at Mount Sinai Medicine showed in a landmark study in *Nature* (2010) that memories transform every time they're recalled. They're malleable and changeable. "To put it in an extreme way, if we are all rewriting our memories every time we recall an event, the memory exists not as a file in our brain but only as the most recent rewrite of a scenario. Every memory is fabricated, and the past is nothing more than our last retelling of it. Archival memory data is mixed with whatever new information helps shape the way we think—and feel—about it." [11]

But...but...wait. Who am I, then?

We are the collection of our memories, aren't we? We're here, in the places we live, because of what we survived to get to these points, and if we can't trust our own memories, then who *are* we?

I like to think of my memories as files in big drawers. Every time I pull one out, I also happen to be covered in my emotional paint of the day. When I look at the memory of finding a banana-seat bicycle under the Christmas tree while I'm having a sad, emotional day of missing my dead mother, the memory gets tinged and changed. It's happening right now, as I type. I'm adding a layer of sadness, of impermanence to it. If I look at the same memory while watching my nephew open his Christmas presents under a different tree, the memory brightens. As I fold the memory away for another day, I'm putting *that* retelling back into the file cabinet. It's not the original. It's a many-times mimeographed idea of that memory.

Which, Schiller says, is sometimes the reason people *don't* want to talk about the past. Her own father is a Holocaust survivor who rarely spoke of that time. Not long ago, he spoke briefly of the family he loved and lost. "Schiller now suspects that her father's reluctance to recall those traumatic events is a way of protecting and preserving memories so beautiful that he wants never to rewrite them and risk losing their power."

Schiller herself believes that the only way to freeze a memory "is to put it into a story."

Which is what we're doing in writing memoir—we're writing the story and nailing it down.

As memoirists, we must proceed with an artistic mix of courage and caution—once you catch your story in words and trap it on the page, it will remain as the ultimate truth forever, even though we know that memories are fallible and changeable.

Then, are we lying?

If we tell stories that might or might not *actually* be true to the exact thing that happened, are we constantly deceiving our readers?

Well, do I have a story for you!

You know how I started this book telling you about the Halloween night my sister and I sat on my porch drinking wine as children ravaged the neighborhood looking for treats—the night she told me about NaNoWriMo, which would change my life?

I was blogging back then (I started in 2002). I rarely look at my old posts, but I wondered if I'd written about finding out about NaNoWriMo.

I searched my site, and I had.

On the twelfth of October, 2006, I wrote about signing up for NaNo. This means my sister told me about it that day or perhaps the day before.

Not on Halloween.

I'm sure that same year we sat on the back porch on Halloween night and listened to the distant screams of children. I know we drank wine. We probably even talked about NaNo, which is perhaps how the timeline got compressed in my memory.

I'm called to tell my "writer's origin story" at least five or six times a year at different writing events. At some point, and I have no idea when this happened, I told the Halloween story and how I learned about NaNo with just one night to pull together an idea for a novel.

This did not happen.

I was tempted to change the beginning of the book, but instead, I decided to leave it in. It's not a cautionary tale—I'm not angry at myself for making this mistake. I leave it in to show that while I was doing the best I could with a memory, I still got it wrong. And I'm admitting it.

Now that I know the truth, I would *not* put the story into a book in which I didn't admit that this wasn't precisely the way it happened. Now that I know I was wrong, I can't tell the story like this again (damn it). But one time, I forgot the truth and put the wrong timeline into a story for telling. By doing that, it cemented it in my mind as the way it happened.

And even though I thought it was a true memory, I was lying when telling it.

I'm okay with that.

Why? Because I didn't set out to deceive anyone. I was attempting to tell the truth. Anytime I find out that I've been wrong, I forgive myself and tell the new, closer-to-truth story.

Two Tools for Honesty

Room Tone:

I think about "room tone" a lot. In TV and movies, this is the sound of a room, measured without other noise happening in it. Sound technicians take this reading so that later they can strip out the ambient noise and isolate the important sounds.

I like to look at room tone from an emotional standpoint. Even if I can't exactly remember everything that happened the afternoon when I learned my friend Eileen had been killed by sharks (true story), even if I can't remember exactly what my best friend's father said, or how we mourned Eileen's death that afternoon, I can remember the tone of the room. It was quiet. Scared. Crushed.

When I recreate dialogue and action, I try to honor the room tone. When I write this scene, what I put on the page must match that tone.

I might not remember exactly what we were eating that afternoon, but I'm pretty sure I wasn't ecstatically chowing down on rainbow-flavored cupcakes. If there was alcohol, it wasn't being lifted triumphantly up for hearty, happy glass clinks. I can use the process of elimination to help me remember what did happen. Mom wouldn't have been cooking. Larry wouldn't have been sober. The church community wouldn't have left us alone with the grief. *Aunt Rose came over with so much adobo we thought there was no chicken left on the island. Larry got steadily drunker, his face lengthening, his jowls stretching to the ground. Dad played morose World War I songs on the guitar until Mom begged him to please, for the love all that's holy, just stop.*

Look at the room tone of the memory you're pulling up. If it's an important memory, one that you want to capture on the page, write down the tone so that you don't overwrite it with some other emotion. And then honor that tone.

Rachael's 80 Percent Rule

The second thing that I advocate doing when writing down memories, be they dialogue or action, is to consider my 80 percent rule.

If you have a memory of a conversation, even if you're not sure word for word what was said, you get to recreate it IF you can be 80 percent (or more) certain that the person saying it would have said it the way you write that they did.

If my father hits his thumb with a hammer, I can be 96 percent sure he'll yell, "God bless America!" I know this because I know him. I haven't memorized everything he's ever said (to his everlasting sadness). But I know that if I inserted this sentence into a scene in which he hurts himself, I'm almost certainly getting it just right.

You know the people you love. You know their syntax, their diction. You know how they react to certain stimuli, and you know how they will *not* react.

Other Liberties Often Taken by Memoirists

In memoir, it's generally considered acceptable to recreate scenes by taking the following kinds of liberties (though you will be the ultimate judge as to whether these feel acceptable to you):

1. Recreating dialogue. Most memoirists do this without feeling the need to say before every scene, "I think it went something like this." As readers, we assume they've said that, as part of the conceit of memoir.

2. Conflating situations/shifting time. It can be extremely tedious and not at all helpful to a story's progression to write down every single time things happened, in the exact order in which they happened. If you went to grad school after taking four trips to see the same campus to try to make up your mind, your reader will be bored stiff if you describe each drive to Berkeley and what you saw there on each subsequent trip. Conflate those four trips and pull out the best parts that illuminate your story structure.

3. Combining/changing characters. If you lived with five male roommates who were all studying to be lawyers and who all drank too much on the weekends, for the love of God, don't tell us about each one of them if they're not pivotal to your story. (If each one is a main character? Then absolutely tell us everything about each one). But if back then *you* could barely tell them apart, we as readers will never have a chance. Create a composite character and tell about the time you got locked on the roof with him. The reader doesn't care that this was George from Indiana, not Ted from Illinois.

4. Moving in time to give information to the reader that you didn't have at the moment being described. If this is the aunt that will kill your grandfather with a shotgun, it's okay to jump forward to say that, even if you're only five years old in the scene and Granddad is still hale and hearty. It's also okay *not* to give that information and withhold it for later. You're in charge here, no one else. Another thing that memoirists do is use a single incident to stand in for a block of time. For example, you can use one episode from a workplace that can stand in for that entire block of seven years you held that job.

5. Disguising features/changing names of characters. *This* is a point at which you get to straight-up lie, which feels very strange indeed. When I was writing a piece about an ex-lover, I made him a novelist instead of a songwriter. I changed his name and his height and his hair. I changed the details of his family and of the car he drove. I did this to protect him, so that no one could point and say, *Hey, is that the guy you're talking about?* We're not in touch—I couldn't run the piece past him, nor would I have actually done so. But in doing this, I was still careful to protect the room tone of my memories of him. I couldn't have made the gentle songwriter I loved into a techie-start-up guy. I honored the way he looked at me, changing nothing about the way his eyes warmed like honey in tea when he caught sight of me across a room. I told the truth about a real person but changed the details to protect him.

Mary Karr says, "Truth may have become a foggy, fuzzy nether area. **But untruth is simple: making up events with the intention to deceive.**" [12] [Emphasis mine.]

The intention to deceive is easy to spot—perhaps not so much in other people's works, nor should we waste time trying to do so, but in our own. When you do a gut check of what you're writing, you'll know. *Am I making this up with the intention to deceive my reader about anything at all? Or am I showing details that I'm more than 80 percent sure happened? Am I preserving the room tone of this memory?*

And honestly, the memoirists I respect the most admit they are fallible. There are so many ways to easily admit that we don't remember things perfectly.

It probably went something like this...

I can imagine that...

I don't remember most of that night, but I remember the feel of my cotton nightgown damp against my legs and the way the clock ticked like it was desperate to get the counting done.

Look at this piece from Hilary Mantel's gorgeous *Giving Up the Ghost*: "It is strange that, though this story awed me, I don't know the end of it. Did my grandfather lean across the room—the room half-lit, half-heated, by a flickering paraffin stove—did he lean out of the shadows, offering his hand? ...I imagine this night, the huddle of men, the railwaymen, their faces turned to the storyteller, their different badges of authority and rank, their silver buttons gleaming against the coarse near-black of their uniforms; some with their lives before them, some with their best years gone. Had he seen too much, the sergeant-instructor, was the time for shake-hands lost? He rose, I believe, from his bench at the back, and walked out unremarked onto the platform, looking up and down the track for the distant wink from the signals, red or green...I see him raise his head, look down the track, narrow his eyes, and exhale; his breath drifts out to join the night, the long blue night of the obscure." [13]

Mantel was not there. She admits she doesn't know how this went. But she imagines it to the best of her ability, and she admits it deftly, weaving her ignorance into her certainty. Because she says it like this, I trust her completely, and I'm willing to believe every word she says.

Memoirist Phillip Lopate says in *To Show and to Tell*, "'I would be more willing to attach myself to the word 'honesty.' We may not ever be in possession of the truth, but at least as nonfiction writers we can try to be as honest as our courage permits. Honest to the world of facts outside ourselves, honest in reporting what we actually felt and did, and finally, honest about our own confusions and doubts." [14]

Tell your honest truth. And overall, err toward kindness.

You can't go wrong if you do that, especially if you're also erring toward judging yourself more harshly than any other character in your memoir.

If that truth is corrected later? You get to correct it for yourself, too. Grant yourself forgiveness and move on. And then write more.

Chapter Six

WHY YOU SHOULD WRITE QUICKLY

This book is about fast-drafting. You've picked up this particular tome because you don't have time to waste. Good for you; of course you don't. We'll talk about how to write fast, but first, we have to address something that everyone worries about.

Writing quickly doesn't mean writing badly.

There, are you relieved? Did you think you'd have to be a hack to want to write something fast? Hack, no!

Except there's just one thing—writing quickly *will* mean writing badly.

And guess what?

Slow writing will *also* include writing badly.

That's just the way writing is, even if you're an incredibly experienced writer with dozens of published books. You start with a first draft full of bad writing, and then you make it better. That's all.

Are you hyperventilating yet? Take a deep breath, do *not*

breathe into a paper bag. (Know why you shouldn't? I worked in emergency services for a long time before I was a full-time writer, and we didn't advocate breathing into a bag because people *choke on receipts*.)

In any case, though, calm down.

You're going to write badly.

YOU ARE GOING TO WRITE BADLY.

First drafts are always terrible, and for new writers, they're particularly painful. There's a really good reason for this.

The Gap

Ira Glass, host of *This American Life*, has a theory about the Gap (the artistic gap, not the place where you get jeans). It was something that explained a lot to me when I was starting out. Let me explain it to you.

As a reader, your taste is already killer. You *know* good writing when you read it. You appreciate it. You drink it in like water, and you love being near, in, and around it.

But as a writer, perhaps you're not quite there yet.

And the bitch of it is that, with your excellent taste, you can tell that what you're making just isn't up to the level you want it to be.

At this point, most writers quit.

Taking more classes doesn't close the gap. Neither does waiting until you become a better writer—it's astonishing how many people wait for this day that will never magically come.

The *only* thing that closes that gap is writing. More writing. Lots and lots and lots of writing. Fast writing! Yeah, sure, we learn from reading, from teachers, from craft books, from consciously thinking about and analyzing our writing. But we learn most of all from doing the work.

We learn most from putting our butts in the chair and writing badly. Every day that you write, you're getting better (this is true —believe it even if you can't feel it yet). That's the beautiful thing. You don't have to *try* to get better, so stop worrying about how to do that. You just get better and better the more you write. Automatically.

So, in this first draft, you'll write badly.

That's okay, though. Susan Sontag said, "What I write is smarter than I am, because I can rewrite it." You'll eventually bring your book up to the level you will recognize as good, but the first draft isn't the time to do it.

Please know this: no one writes a book that doesn't need revision. Not one single person does that, and they never have. If anyone ever tells you that they did, first, call them a liar to their face, and then have them email me so I can tell them the same thing.

Some people do revise as they go along. In my entire two-decade career, I've met two (TWO!) people for whom this works. They make their words as perfect as they can before they go on to write more, and they produce clean manuscripts by the end of the draft. Keep in mind, though, this isn't actually their first draft; they've just been revising as they go in mini-revision sessions.

I've found that almost all new writers *think* this is their method. They write, they clean it up, they move a little further forward, and they clean it up more.

Most people get stuck right there.

They have a gorgeous first five or fifty pages. But they can't move forward. That's because something's already gone wrong, and because they're so wedded to these perfect pages, they can't go back and figure out what's got them stuck. They can't see the problem in the forest because those trees look so damn *good*.

You know why this happens?

Revising as you go isn't the right process for most people.

I am pretty damn willing to die on this hill. The right process for most writers is to write a fast, terrible draft.

In essence, while writing quickly, you're throwing the clay on the pottery wheel. It takes time to get the big, wet, clay lump to stick. You have to push and pull at it to get it all on there. Then you have to center it, making sure it's balanced. It's a lot of hard, heavy work getting all the material in place.

But once it's in place? *Then* you can start shifting it around, making it into the actual gorgeous form you already know is in there.

So here's the plain truth: if you think you're a perfectionist who must revise as you go, this is your best process ONLY if you're doing it this way AND completing books you're proud of. (The *and* must be there.)

But if, like most writers, you *think* this is your process but you have a bunch of stalled attempts at memoirs or novels on your hard drive, then revising as you go is *not* your process.

The only thing that will break you free is to allow yourself to write a terrible draft and fix it later.

We'll talk more about getting out of your own way later, but for now, let's talk about what a memoir looks like.

How Long is a Memoir?

We've already learned that memoirs are arranged by either theme or time.

The next question is always, *How long is a memoir, anyway?*

It's a good question, and like all good questions, it's hard to answer. Memoir length varies.

Personally, I think in terms of word count, as most people in publishing do. You can also think in pages, but since word count can vary by the font and page size, word count is a better absolute measure. Industry-wise, a page is accepted to be 250 words. So, when I say 10,000 words, that's forty pages.

A short memoir can run from 25,000 to 40,000 words. A medium one will be 40,000-80,000 words, and a long one will be anything over that. If you're hoping to take a traditional publishing route with one of the Big Five American publishing houses, you'll have to aim for medium or longer, up to about 100,000 words. Anything longer than that raises eyebrows.

If you're thinking of self-publishing, though, you can do whatever the heck you want. You could publish a short-story-length memoir, just five or ten pages, or you could produce a magnum opus of 200,000 words and call yourself the George R. R. Martin of memoir.

Most of my students who complete their memoirs find themselves in the 40,000-60,000 word range. That seems to be a sweet spot: long enough to cover everything and get the reader truly invested in the world, short enough to actually finish.

Doing the Math

Getting writing done comes down to simple arithmetic, my friends. Your math teacher was right. I'm sorry about that.

Let's say your memoir will be 45,000 words—on the shorter side of medium length because we want to get this done quickly so that we can have a terrible first draft that we can shape into something really great.

In this book, you'll learn methods of writing quickly. I can reliably write 2,000 words an hour without trying too hard, but I've been at this game a long time. When you start, it might be a stretch to get even 500 words done in the same amount of time.

So here's a little assignment for you. This exercise might blow your mind, so I really encourage you to get up off the couch or out of the bed (yes, I told you I can see you) and *try* this.

Exercise:

Fifteen Minute Mad Dash:

Go to your computer and write for fifteen minutes, as fast as you can. Set an alarm on your phone. *KEEP YOUR HANDS MOVING.* When you run out of things to type (and you will), push yourself to keep going. Lost that train of thought? That's fine! That happens! Jump on the next train and ride it to a different destination.

Yes, you're typing this, not handwriting it, as I assume you'll write your memoir in some kind of word-processing app. (If not, you might not be fast-drafting, but you can certainly still hand-write a memoir.)

Your prompt will be "Home is..." but keep reading before starting.

Your stab at this exercise can include describing the last five places you resided. It can be about a person who means home to you. It can be about the couch that says you're finally off work. It can be about the home you always wanted, or the one you had and lost. If you're writing about one kind of home and run out of words, then *restart the sentence* and chase it.

DO NOT GO BACK AND READ AS YOU WRITE. This is key! You can back up to fix a quick spelling error if you haven't gone more than a word or two past it. But don't read! Don't stop! Keep the hands moving! You can fix everything later!

Your prompt: *Home is...* **Do this for fifteen minutes exactly. Start now.**

All done?

Do the math. Check your word count and multiply that by four. This is your average words-per-hour. Don't be alarmed if you're under five hundred words per hour. *Do* be surprised (and brag to a friend!) if you're over a thousand.

Your rate will go up, I promise you, as you get used to putting crappy words on the page. They won't stay crappy. You'll fix them later. For this draft, we just get out of the way and write.

So let's look at that 45,000 word memoir of yours now that you know your own personal word per hour rate.

It's normal to start slowly, but you'll quickly break the 1000 word per hour (WPH) rate as you get used to this fast-draft method. You'll also have a plan, a roadmap for your memoir (more on that to come).

Forty-five thousand words equals 40-45 hours of work, not including good old thinkin' time. Your plotting and planning time will only be a couple or three hours. I could let you have more time, but you and I both know the truth: if I gave you thirty hours to plot your memoir, you could fill it. Parkinson's Law says, "Work expands to fill the time available for its completion." Similarly, if I gave you just thirty minutes to plan your whole memoir, you could do that, too.

It generally takes me between one to six months to write a first draft. And in obvious-but-still-surprising news, it always takes *the exact same amount* of butt-in-chair-hands-on-keyboard time, whether I spread that over one month or twenty. I keep careful track of how my time is spent, and it takes about fifty hours for me to produce a 95,000 word novel, no matter how many days those hours are spread over.

So this is a good time to talk about writing fatigue and deep work.

Deep Work

Sadly, you can't do normal-person math for how you'll fit in those writing hours. *Fifty hours to write a full novel? Why, that's less than a week of eight-hour days!*

Nope, nope, *nope.*

Writing takes deep work. Cal Newport, the author of *Deep Work*, describes this as "the ability to focus without distraction on a cognitively demanding task. It's a skill that allows you to quickly master complicated information and produce better results in less time. Deep work will make you better at what you do and provide the sense of true fulfillment that comes from craftsmanship. In short, deep work is like a super power in our increasingly competitive twenty-first century economy. And yet, most people have lost the ability to go deep—spending their days instead in a frantic blur of email and social media, not even realizing there's a better way." [15]

As we work deeply without distraction, our skills are cemented as myelin is built around neurons. The more myelination our neurons build, the better we get at the skill, and the longer we can do it (up to that upper limit).

And no one, even the top experts in their fields, can reliably do more than three to four hours of deep work at a time.

Read that again.

No one, even the top experts in their fields, can reliably do more than three to four hours of deep work at a time.

Hearing that was *such* a relief to me.

Personally, I can do two to three hours, max, in full deep-work mode. After that, I'm good to keep working for the rest of the day, but I need to tackle other, lighter tasks like email and marketing.

Don't forget, just thinking is mentally *and* physically demanding. You'll feel it in your body, not just your brain. It's a good feeling—I love when I stand up from the desk and my brain is mush and my body just wants a nap. You feel used up, and it's nice. You did this to yourself. You left tracks behind you on the page. You're a *writer*.

So, What's Normal?

There's no such thing as normal (thank God), but many professional writers aim for 1000-2000 words a day. NaNoWriMo wrests 1,667 words from you daily. When I'm first-drafting a book, my goal is always 2000 words a day, five days a week (I try to take weekends off though that's not always doable). My goal can get pushed up to 4000 words a day when I'm running up against a deadline. Anything more than 4000 tends to leave me wobbly and strung-out, an overcooked writing noodle with very little ability to speak English cogently. (My wife always knows when I've had a massive writing day because I ask her to do things like weed the frogs instead of feed the dogs. The melting of your brain out your ears is common when you hit high word counts. Revel in your tongue-tiedness.)

But normal can simply be:

- Writing regularly without distractions.
- Writing toward a daily word goal.
- Believing that your writing is getting better (even when it feels like it's not).
- Knowing that every word you write gets you closer to the finish line.

Perhaps you already know that you'll be comfortable writing 1000 words a day, three days a week. Great! Now you know you can write your memoir in fifteen weeks.

Do the math to figure out your pace. There's lots more on pacing and going quickly in the *How to Get Out of Your Own Way and Write* section, but don't jump there yet! We have a bit more to think about first.

Now let's talk about *your* specific memoir.

Chapter Seven

TYPES OF MEMOIR

There are *so* many different kinds of memoir within the genre that it's impossible to list them all here, but here are a few for you to think about. While you're going over this list, ask yourself what's *your* favorite kind to read? Can you write that kind? Personally, my favorite kind is the pastoral memoir, but since my wife and I are city girls and won't be moving to live off the land any time in the near future, I'm currently writing my second-favorite kind, the stunt memoir (a year of refilling the creative well, each month focused on a different theme).

Types of Memoirs:

List inspired by and expanded upon from Swenson Book Development.

- Celebrity, athletic, political, or public figure: Famous people writing well-paid and well-publicized books, usually ghost-written.

- Travel: The story of a trip or trips. *Eat Pray Love* fits into this category.
- Spiritual: The story of finding a spiritual revelation. *Eat Pray Love* also fits into this category, immediately proving the fact that it's okay to hit more than one category.
- Food: *Julie and Julia* fits in here, as does, you guessed it, *Eat Pray Love*. Is Elizabeth Gilbert just showing off now?
- Grief: Joan Didion's *The Year of Magical Thinking* and Sonali Deraniyagala's *Wave* are good examples.
- Animal: Yep, there are plenty of memoirs about a pet that was pivotal to a life. I have to admit to a weakness for these, although the end of the book is usually that the animal died, so ouch.
- Farmsteading/Pastoral: A person for whom free-range eggs are as close as they get to a farm suddenly up and moves to the country, preferably with their long-suffering spouse whose subsequent horror can be mined for comic effect.
- Mommy Dearest/Growing Up Dysfunctional: These books are full of family pain and are sometimes hard to read. *The Glass Castle* fits here. Care should be taken to add some humor/irreverence, or your reader will want to kill himself with a bread knife by the end.
- Escape From Religious Extremism: Sign me up! I'm always down for a cult memoir. Bonus points if the setting is something I'm not familiar with, like a jungle. Or, okay, a church.
- I'll Take You There (Zeitgeist): These capture the spirit of a time. Here, care has to be taken to bring the author into the narrative. It's easy to get lost in a Summer of Love memory and talk a lot about Janis Joplin, but Janis (bless her) will never be as

interesting to the reader as *you* will be. Front and center, please.

- I Will Survive (Disaster): Did you cut off your leg to get away from a rabid panda? This is your genre!
- Love and Romance: Guess what fits here? Yep, that damn *Eat Pray Love*. I'm telling you, I'm starting to figure out why this book was as big as it was.
- Family and Friendship Relationships: *Let's Take the Long Way Home* by Gail Caldwell, or Ann Patchett's *Truth and Beauty* are good examples.
- Workplace or Career/business: Here, the business should be something interesting. If you set out to write the story of your life seen through the Excel spreadsheets you edited, you might be signing yourself up for difficulty (though I'm sure it can be done well in the right hands). But if you train killer whales to be international spies? We sure want to hear about it.
- Exploration or Adventure: Did you get lost hiking in Peru? Tell us about what you saw. This can strongly overlap with Travel or Disaster memoirs.
- Illness: Your everyday cancer memoir fits in here. Yes, there are lots of them. Yes, agents are tired of getting queried about them. No, that doesn't mean that yours isn't the one the world is waiting for. It's possible that your illness memoir will be the one that helps someone else find their way through, so yes, write it if you're called to it.
- Addiction/recovery: Again, sign me up. If you were ever too strung-out on meth to remember to pick your kid up from school, I want to read your book. What? I'm a simple person. I like the reminder that my problems aren't that bad. Memoir is a great way to be reminded of this.
- Humor: Caitlyn Moran's *How to Be a Woman*. David

Sedaris's whole catalog. Humor isn't easy to write, but I think you know if you're good at it. And if you're great at it, it might be difficult to write anything but.

- Call to Action: Often (but not always) political, call to action memoirs are the ones that get you off your ass and talk you into *doing* something. Ta-Nehesi Coates's *Between the World and Me* is a recent stunning example of this.

- Stunt: As mentioned, when a memoirist does something in order to write about it. Anything by A.J. Jacobs is in this category, like the time he tried to live by all biblical rules for a year, or when he took a year to read the encyclopedia.

Exercise:

What kind of memoir are you drawn to writing? Where does your germ of an idea fit in this list? Again, you can combine aspects from these, but overall, you should know what category best fits the idea you're flipping around in your mind. If you think yours fits into two or more categories, write them all down.

Now, narrow it down a bit if you have several: which one are you *most* drawn to writing? Your book might fit into both Travel and Recovery, but what will your actual focus of the book be? Which one makes your heart race? There will be one category you sway toward a bit more than the other. Write this one down. Circle it. Kiss the page if you want to. You're headed that way.

Chapter Eight

PLANNING: PART ONE

Let's go back to the beginner's mind for a moment.

It's possible this is where you already live—maybe this whole writing idea is new to you, and you're taking all of this in with great big eyes and a Christmas-morning wonderment.

But it's just as possible that you're an old hand at this writing gig. Maybe you've already written some fiction. Perhaps you've taken a lot of writing classes, or you're in an MFA program somewhere.

For now, let go of what you know.

I know that's difficult, but a person who already feels like a master of writing has a hard time coming to anything new—their minds are closed, and they see less opportunity for creativity.

A beginner, though, doesn't know what's possible and what's not; therefore, she can push past impossible and make something truly spectacular happen.

If you have expectations, let them go. Let them hit the floor next to you. If you're a popular science fiction author, and you're worried that this new memoir has to look or act a certain way to please your readers, try to put that to the side.

Your memoir can be *anything* you want it to be.

Starting Small

Small steps lead to great leaps. We want to make sure your memoir has a narrative arc (also known as a story arc). Again, you're not going to write a strictly chronological report of things that happened to you, even if you're writing a time-based memoir. You're going to structure your scenes into a format that is most pleasing to a reader, because, honestly, this is all about them. *You* already know your story. You're not retelling it so *you* can get high off the fumes of your own past—you want to intoxicate your reader, instead.

You're retelling your tale so that you can share it with someone. I've yet to have a single person in one of my classes say that they are writing a memoir to show to absolutely no one, ever. Often they *can't* show their work to anyone—it's either too painful or too scary to do so. But even in the most timid heart of hearts, they're still writing this for an outside reader: a sibling, a daughter, a grandson, or even that nebulous unknown person who might find their writing after the author's death.

Readers don't only expect a story arc. They *need* it. We'll talk a lot more about this soon, but first, a few baby steps.

What we're searching for is a general idea about the direction you want to take your memoir.

This is super important, y'all. If you get into your car in Austin and start to drive, it's useful to know whether you're heading to New York City or San Francisco. You don't have to know much more if your trip is that long (my basic concerns center around the best places to stop for Corn Nuts and Krispy Kreme donuts), but you should be able to decide which point of the compass to head for.

Exercise:

Your Six Pivotal Moments

Grab your pen.

A Note on Exercises:
    When I ask you to grab your pen and write something down, I mean it. Don't be like me. I like to read writing books and not do any of the exercises and then get irritated when the magic doesn't rub off on me. But seriously, the magic only works when you show up. And let me add you don't actually have to get up out of bed (I told you, I see you) to go to the computer or go to the kitchen to find a pen. I bet your phone is within arm's reach. Is it? Great. Open to a text notepad and get ready. Reading on the Kindle app on your phone? Or on your Paperwhite? Hold down the words to highlight them and ADD A NOTE right inside. Bam! You're writing! Writers write. That's all you have to do. You can find those Kindle notes by going to read.amazon.com/notebook. iBooks has a similar feature. You just ran out of excuses to not do this, didn't you?

So, going back to what I was saying before I CALLED YOU OUT:
    Grab your pen or get ready to note right within this book.

Write down the six pivotal moments that shaped you as a human. Yes, I want six. No more, and importantly, no fewer. This exercise is about culling down ideas.

Frequently, people list things like:

- Childbirth
- Loss of a loved one
- Job (acquisition or loss)
- Marriage
- Moving to a new place

Personally, the six things that shaped me most are:

- My mother's death
- Marriage
- My move to Oakland, California
- My 911 job
- Writing my first book
- Publication

They didn't happen in this order, and that's okay. Write down your six in any order that they occur to you.

If you have more than six, decide which had a bigger impact. Your brother's death may not have been as impactful as your grandmother's death—even though that's unexpected, this is about *your* truth. You get to decide what's most important. There's no judging. You won't show this list to anyone else. Be honest with yourself.

Okay, got them? Great. Let's move on to the next step.

The Six-Word Memoir

Ernest Hemingway is popularly said to have been challenged to write a six-word complete story. *For sale, baby shoes, never worn.* It's apocryphal—no one knows if he actually did write this—but wow, it's a good one, right? It's all there. You know the hope and the heartbreak, the beginning, middle, and end, just from those six little words.

Inspired by this, in 2006, the online storytelling magazine, *Smith,* challenged their readers to tell their stories in just six words. It became hugely popular, spawning multiple book collections and inspiring writers around the globe.

The six-word memoir is a simple form. Your story, in six words. It's easy enough that second-graders understand it, and tricky enough that award-winning poets struggle with it.

Yes, the six-word memoir really a memoir.

And yes, you can have as many of them as you like, just like full-length memoirs (but the six-word version is practically instant and therefore gratifying).

But Rachael, how on earth do I distill the essence of who I am into just six words?

That's the magic of this! You can, just as you can distill your life into a full-length memoir. But this way is a lot faster and almost as much fun.

Whenever I set my students this task, I redo my own six-word memoirs. Here are a few that I've penned just for this occasion.

- Letters, words, sentences: my life's grammar.
- Make, break, fix. Do it again.
- Arrived with hope, leaving with same.

Exercise:

Write a six-word memoir of your own.

Stumped? Look at your six pivotal moments. Choose one and write about that. If your divorce was a pivotal moment, write a six-word memoir about it, keeping the focus on yourself. *Married too young. Divorced just right.*

Be loose and floppy with your attempt. If your shoulders go high, if your jaw starts to clench as you furiously scratch out word after word because they're not just right, slow down and take a deep breath. You're not going to get this wrong. You can't. It's yours. Grab it.

Write it down.

Then do another one.

Go for three.

Feeling the rush? Do some more. Write one for every pivotal point, then add a couple more. Finish when you're depleted of ideas, but don't work at this for more than ten minutes.

(Want to share? Go to Twitter and hashtag yours #sixwordmemoir.)

What's the *point* of writing a six-word memoir?

Some wise guy in class always challenges me on this, wanting to do more and go faster, hoping that this exercise is trivial and that he won't have to do it.

But this exercise is about distillation. In chemistry, you separate liquids with different boiling points by heating them until one becomes vapor. The vapor is caught by a condenser, and it's brought back to liquid, only by then, instead of being mixed with something else, it's purely itself.

This exercise is purely *you*. No one can write your six-word memoirs.

I like to think of these like a tombstone epitaph: something that could fit on a grave marker. I'm a little macabre that way, as many writers are. Writing is its own way of leaving a mark on the world. Most "normal" people don't get that many opportunities to write what they mean. They might scribble a bit online, but that's ephemeral and forgotten quickly. The average life of a Tweet, for example, is fifteen minutes. A Facebook post's average life is five hours. After that, the chance of being read plummets.

But leaving behind actual writing for the people who love you to find? That's something rare and precious, and it's worth even more if you're perfectly truthful.

The six-word memoir gets you to distill what's most important to *you*. It's yours, completely. You don't have to fit anyone else into this exercise.

To that point, try to be alone in at least one of your six-word memoirs. If every single six-word memoir you've come up with so far shows you as a mother of two small children or a wife or an employee, write another one in which you're featured alone, the only actor in this tiny play of your life.

Done?

Good for you. It was more fun than you thought it would be, right? To me, this exercise scratches the counting-on-fingers itch of haiku, but instead of writing about the beauty of nature, you get to write about yourself.

And more than that, you're writing about the very most important part of yourself. Even if you show no one this work, you know in your heart that your six-word memoirs capture you as the incredible, unique, one-of-a-kind person you are.

In these, you capture some of your life's main points. Yes, points, plural. You are a multitude of collected things.

But one of those six-word stories is the one you'll write about for your memoir.

Just one.

So get out your pen again and draw a big star next to the one you think you want to write about.

This will be your focus.

This will be your *book*.

IMPORTANT:

This can change! As you work forward in this book, you might decide that instead of writing about your life as seen through the wedding cakes you've baked, you want to write about your year surfing in Tonga. That's *fine*. I'm not going to come to your house and rap your knuckles for changing your mind. But we do this—pick one single angle—at this point for a very real reason.

Creativity Within Constraints

If you came to me and paid me to tell you what to write about, and I said, "Write a novel," you'd be frustrated and overwhelmed. A novel? A novel is huge! How are you supposed to write a novel? Where do you even start? You'd stalk away from me and go sit on the curb and throw pebbles into the street, imagining that you were aiming each rock at my head.

But if I said to you, "Write a novel about a boxing ring manager who was born with only one arm who lives in Aspen and is in love with a pharmaceutical rep who doesn't know he's alive," you might be annoyed with me because you don't care a single bit about boxing, but you'd be able to write it. You'd be able to come up with a starting place: an old building in downtown Aspen that our hero can imagine full of, um...boxing equipment. (Were I to write this book, it would obviously take a little research.) You can imagine the end: he wins the girl, dipping her with his one arm, kissing her till the lights come up.

Giving yourself constraints for memoir works the same way. To write the story of your life? It's terrifying to even think about starting.

But to write the story that's held up by your favorite six-word memoir?

Yes.

You can do this.

Chapter Nine

PLANNING: PART TWO

Now you've got your six-word memoir.

You've distilled the essence of what you think you might write about (again, I provide the gentle reminder that this can change; there's no need for panic).

Now let's expand it back out a little bit.

Your Big Personal Change

In any story, whether it's fiction or memoir, the main character needs to undergo change.

And guess who the main character is in your memoir? Yep, it's you.

So you, in the pages of your memoir, *have to change*. You must show how you began, and where you ended up, and those two points must be different.

Change is essential to your book.

Why? Because that's what we want as humans.

We arrive on this earth kind of stupid. You have to admit it.

We can't walk or talk. We can't even hold a cell phone for the first few months of our lives. But we change. We grow and expand (especially in our forties! *tugs belt*). Stasis is boring. Change is interesting. We learn from other's experiences, and we crave watching others adapt to what happens to them. Plus, hearing another person pontificate about how cool they are and how they've always been that way is deadly dull. You don't feel like reading that book, do you?

Besides being boring, though, the lack of change in a character shows that we can't trust the narrator (guess what? That's also you —we'll talk later about how the main character and narrator are different). As readers—as media consumers in the Western Hemisphere—we've been trained to expect character change. If your book opens with you as a broke single mother living on food stamps, we expect you to end up in a different situation by the end. It doesn't have to be the opposite. You don't have to end up a married mother, dripping diamond tennis bracelets. But it has to shift in an important way.

So, look at your six-word memoir.
   Really think about it.
   Then fill in these blanks:
   I started out _____.
   I ended up _____.

These don't need to be fancy or long or even well-written sentences. This big personal change just needs to be caught.

Some examples from past students:

- I started out alone in a family that couldn't understand me. I ended up part of a family that loves me as I am.
- I started out thinking I would never make my father

    proud. I ended up realizing I never needed his
    approval.

- I started out broke. I ended up rich.
- I started out rich and miserable. I ended up broke but happy.

Now do yours.

Use your six-word memoir for inspiration. Again, don't spend more than ten minutes on this. Trust your gut.

Got it? This is your character arc throughout this memoir that you'll be writing. Good job.

The Two-Sentence Premise

We're almost done with all the planning that comes before your outline! Hang in here with me—this will be worth it, I promise.

Check out your six-word memoir. Like it? Turn it around in your mind, hold it up to the light. Want to swap out some words? Go for it.

Now set it back down.

Look at your big personal change (also known as your character arc). It's okay to change these words around, but hey, if it ain't too broke, let's charge ahead without fixing it. You can always go back and repeat these steps if you feel like you did them wrong, but you probably didn't. Your first answer is often the best answer.

Now, I want you to think about the book you're going to be writing.

Oh, isn't that idea just so delicious in itself? You're going to do it! And if you were suddenly trapped in a small space with an agent you thought might like to represent your book, what would you say?

The elevator pitch (literally called that so that you can deploy it in an elevator should you ever need to—these are the lines that will make that agent or editor *desperate* to read your book, even if you only have floors 1 to 17 with them) is an important piece of information to have at your disposal after you're done writing. It's a great tool to help you to sell the book.

But the real power of an elevator pitch (also known as a logline) comes from knowing it *before* you write. Is it interesting enough that you want to write a book based on it? Do you think it'll pique the interest of others? Does it excite you to think about?

Before I wrote my memoir *A Life in Stitches*, this is what I would have said if asked for my elevator pitch: "Um, it's about the fact that I'm a knitter? I knit all the time. I guess I'm a really big knitter. Soooo..." *waves a scarf in progress under the poor agent's nose, gets ready to cry into it later*

Now, of course, I know what it is:

A Life in Stitches is the story of my life, loss, and happiness as seen through the sweaters that were on my knitting needles at the time. In it, I show how grief can be managed and joy can be found by the simple act of rubbing two sticks and a piece of string together.

See?

Short and sweet. I can memorize this and stutter it out to an agent even if the elevator ride is only two floors. (And there's always the emergency stop button. Don't tell anyone I told you that.)

Your Turn

You're going to write your two-sentence elevator pitch, keeping your six-word memoir and your big personal change (your character arc) in mind. Yes, this is hard. But stand back and squint and see that you're doing something *really* exciting. You're writing the premise of the entire book, and then you'll write the book that will prove this premise true.

Some sample student two-sentence elevator pitches:

- Born to parents who didn't want me but kept me anyway, it wasn't until I was a mother myself that I learned what a parent's love should be. My children reshaped me into the person I was always meant to be.
- During my high school years, my parents were missionaries of a small cult that tried to convert the people visiting New York City, one tourist at a time. In those four years, I learned exactly what I wanted from life and, more importantly, what I didn't.
- When I survived a plane crash, I realized that the corporate life I'd successfully built around myself didn't matter. I'd never be safe until I stopped trying to control everything and everyone around me.
- I couldn't stop shopping until I ran out of money. When I did, I ran into myself.

Do you see how these work? They don't have to be long—the last one is just long enough to cover the basics. That's all you need.

Write yours now, keeping in mind your six-word memoir and your change (your character arc). Keep messing around with this. Shove the words to the right and then to the left. Make them dance on the page. Play. Explore. Brainstorm. Try to do this by yourself, if possible—know that this is *yours*. You don't have to tell a single person what you're planning to do.

Do this now, and don't spend more than fifteen minutes on it.

Got it?

(DID YOU DO IT? I TOLD YOU I CAN SEE YOU!)

Do you like your two-sentence premise? Are those sentences *yours*? Can you commit to taking this idea further? Do these two sentences again if you're not excited as heck to plunge into this. If the idea is boring to you now, it's not the right idea. There will be *plenty* of time to get bored with your idea later (and it will happen). But right now, in this moment, these two sentences should make you feel a fizzing inside. They should make you scrabble around on your desk for a pen. You should salivate when you think about catching them on paper.

They should feel exciting to you.

They might not feel comfortable, mind you. You might be writing about heavy shit. That's okay.

And these sentences might not feel perfect to you. They could still be rough, or even just not quite right. You might not be sure *how* they're not right, but you can feel it.

Again, it's okay if you change your mind later, about any part of this. But don't let the voice of worry plague you now—those two sentences might not *ever* be perfect (welcome to writing, where each sentence could always be better!).

It's enough that they're done and that they excite you enough to move to the next step.

Okay! Let's do our *final* bit of planning.

Chapter Ten

OUTLINE: THE MOST IMPORTANT PART OF YOUR PLAN

First, make a pot of tea. Or if you're more of a coffee person, brew up a carafe. Whatever shape your thinking cap is in, put it on your head.

It's go time.

You can do this exercise on your laptop or computer, certainly, but unless you have repetitive strain injury (RSI) issues and can't write by hand, I'd suggest starting your outline with pen and paper. There might be a lot of scratching out and arrows happening in a moment, and there's something really rich about having the topography of those decisions visible.

You're going to outline your book now.

Don't be frightened—no one will judge your work to see if you got the roman numerals in the right place. This is just for you.

And magically, this is where your memoir truly becomes *yours*. If, by some completely random accident, you ended up with the exact same two-sentence premise as someone else in the world (and I can almost guarantee this won't happen, ever), your outline will be the proof that your book is as unique as you are. No two will be the same. In fact, no two will even be very similar.

Got your notebook? (Go get it.) Let's do this!

Number one through ten down the left-hand side of your page.

This is your number of chapters. Ten is a really great place to start. You may end up with seven chapters when you're done, or you might have thirty-five. But ten is our jumping-off number.

Now write down some things that happened to you while moving from your early, unchanged self toward the self you want to show at the end of the book. (I say this carefully because the person you become at the end of this memoir might not actually be the person you are today. If, for example, you're only writing about your high school years, the person you are now might be very different from the person you ended up being back then. That's fine. The important part is knowing how you changed over that time and showing that throughout this memoir.)

Write down the big events that mattered on this journey. Slap them down in order, chronologically. (We'll talk later about whether you'll keep this order—don't worry about other structures right now.)

Got ten? (Or eight, or twelve?)

Next step:
Write two or three smaller things that contributed to each big event that happened.

What the hell does that mean, Rachael?

For example, Stella's memoir is about the year she spent trying to stay in love with a person who should have been a one-night stand.

- Her six-word memoir: Love is a choice? Oh, crap.
- Her Big Personal Change: I started out thinking I needed someone to make me whole. I ended up happy to be alone.
- Her Two-Sentence Elevator Pitch: I thought I could pick who I fell in love with, and that if I tried hard enough, he'd fall in love with me back. After a year of struggling to love someone who didn't deserve it, I learned to be in love with myself instead.

Stella's Outline (*just three points instead of ten—you'll get the picture*)

1. The first time I met Dave.

A. The way I got dragged to the hookah bar by coworkers convinced it was the best place ever.

B. The night itself, how we danced and then I went to his place.

C. The morning after, when I ran away without leaving any info behind.

2. Our first real date.

A. The romance of him tracking me down, the way he got my phone number only after promising Elise he'd be good to me forever.

B. Eating on board the bay cruise boat.

C. The way he looked later that night, the way I thought, "I'm going to choose to love this person, whether he likes it or not."

3. Shacking up.

A. Leaving my roommate behind.

B. Elise pissed off, showdown at Starbucks.

C. Mom refusing to come to the housewarming.

Do you see how this works? Stella is writing about a year with this man. We can assume that her next big events will include things like their first fight, the time she realized Dave would never love her back, breaking up, and moving out.

Under each big event, she lists smaller events that contributed to the larger event.

Big events are *chapters.*

The smaller events will be *scenes.*

Ten chapters, each with three scenes of approximately 1500 words (a healthy, sensible length for a scene) equal a 45,000 word book.

Go ahead and jot down those scenes now. It's totally okay if you have to leave some blanks. You're playing right now.

Don't spend more than thirty minutes doing this.

But, but, but...

I restrict the time on this for a specific reason: you could spend months on just this step. But you don't get to.

We're fast-drafting. That means sometimes we won't do everything as perfectly as we could have, given a much longer time frame. But that's okay because, first, we can fix it later, and second, you'll actually *complete* your memoir, something you've never managed to do before.

Chapter/Scene Length

This is always one of the first things students ask me: How long should my chapter be? How long is a scene?

Great question. Again, it's impossible to give a hard and fast answer.

You get to make this choice. I read a memoir in which each chapter was just a page (this was a rather poetic choice, and because the writer was a poet, it worked beautifully). Other memoirs have chapters that are only one scene each, and each one is less than 1500 words. Other writers set down incredibly long chapters with no scene breaks at all. Again, this is your choice, no one else's. It will depend on your writing voice (more on this later).

But I'll give you my opinion, and it's just that: scenes read easily and well when they're approximately 1200-1800 words long. A scene this long is a manageable size to read in a short amount of time—before falling to sleep, or on a daily commute. And the reason I like to have two or three scenes within a chapter is that those scenes prop up the *idea* of the chapter, proving it.

That said, if you'd like to write a 45,000 word memoir and have sixty scenes of 750 words each and call each one a chapter, you can absolutely do that. You can also have no chapters or scene breaks at all, though that might be a bit confusing for your reader. (Is your brain spinning yet? That's normal, don't worry.)

Now, go back to your outline.

Play with it. Move things around if you feel like it. Try collapsing an event or expanding another one. You aren't making a deal with the devil here. If you decide to change things later, you can, at any point.

Try not to judge your outline too harshly, either. Outlines are ugly things, really. They hold a lot of potentialities, but they are inherently *boring*. You thought that about Stella's example, above, right? Of course, you did. Baldly stated facts on a page *are* boring.

But when Stella dives in and describes that hookah bar around her, the way his eyes met hers and it felt like she'd just been pushed into a cold swimming pool, or when she tells you how it felt to run her fingers across Dave's lips while he slept, the boring facts disappear, and we're transported into her world.

When your scenes are written—no matter how cold and flat they appear in your outline—they become real and beautiful.

Let this exercise remind you that yes, you really *do* have a book in you.

You've got some scenes you think you could write. You might not have a full ten chapters with thirty scenes, but hey, if you've got even a few, that's a great starting point. And more will come to you as we go, I promise.

Onward!

Chapter Eleven

STORY STRUCTURE AND CHARACTER ARC

You've got an outline now! Congratulations!

Let's talk about how to rip that apart.

You've probably heard of the three-act structure, even if this is your first foray into writing. Stories have a beginning, a middle, and an end. This has been around in Western civilization since the time of Aristotle. From something as short as a joke to as long as an epic fantasy, we can see beginnings and middles and ends in all the stories we enjoy.

Even in memoir (especially in memoir!), we want to consider story structure. Sure, you could write a collection of essays around a theme and argue that they stand together as a collection without thinking about story structure, but I'm going to argue that while that might be true, your collection of essays will be *so much stronger* and more moving to your reader if you consider story structure when you're working on your outline.

Structure and Formula

Most human beings have two arms, two legs, and one head. Of course, there are people born differently, but the vast majority of people *you* know have two arms, two legs, and one head. Within this bodily framework, no two people of all the 108.2 billion people who have ever lived have been exactly alike. They're all different. Unique. This body structure, it could be argued, is formulaic (why don't my friends have tails? Or two heads?) *or* it could be said it's just universal law. Spiders require eight legs. Computer programming requires math. People require skeletons. Stories require structure.

Now, a lot of writers write their first books without thinking too clearly about structure, and this is for a very good reason: we all know what structure is, deep in our bones. We are raised with the three-act structure; we are surrounded by it. Every movie, every sitcom, almost every novel you've ever read—they all use the three-act structure. You're used to *feeling* it around you. As a consumer, we don't know exactly what we want right in the middle of a movie, but when the midpoint turn happens, it releases a flood of dopamine in our minds as our unnamed expectation is met.

You want to do that for your reader, even though, unless she's a writer or in film production, she won't know what she's looking for.

My first novel accidentally got this right. A pantser back then (a person who writes flying by the seat of their pants, without a charted-out plan), I winged that NaNoWriMo novel. And by sheer accident mixed with intuition, I had it all in there. I had a first plot point, pinch points, a context-shifting midpoint, a crisis, and a resolution. It all worked, which helped me sign my agent. The fact that the plot worked well was also a key ingredient in selling the novel to my publisher.

But have you ever heard about the second-book blues? Oh, yeah. This is a very real thing, and it's terrifying. You write your first book over the course of years. No one in New York publishing is waiting for it. No one is banging on your door asking if you're done yet.

But my second book was due—under contract—six months after my first book was. So I had six months to write a book. Sure, I could do it! I thought I could, anyway. I'd done it once; I could surely do it again, right?

I couldn't.

I *did* turn in a book on time. I'm not the kind of person who misses a deadline. I'll drag myself out of my migraine bed, vomit three times, and still make sure my article is turned in on time. So I sent my editor a book.

The next week, I got a phone call from that same editor.

I stood in my workplace parking lot as I spoke to her, balancing on the side of a curb. I watched my black boots flex against the concrete. "Tell me."

"Your writing is strong, and so are your characters. But you need a plot." She sounded kind, but the words ripped out my heart.

"Can I fix it?" Of course I could. I could fix anything, couldn't I? I had talent, right? Was that enough? I just needed her to say it, needed that reassurance.

"Well..." There was a long, terrible pause. "I have to tell you, it's going to take a lot of heavy lifting."

It was all she said. I sat on the curb, the feeling gone from my legs. It was a polite way for her to say, *I don't know. You might not be able to fix this. You screwed up.*

That weekend, I went to a hostel on the coast, alone. I sat at the big, empty dining room table, laid out the pages, and desperately Googled "how to revise a novel." Now, looking back, it seems rather romantic that I took myself, my broken heart, and my failed book to a cheap, private, seaside room with a shared bath to figure out how to save my embryonic career.

But it didn't feel romantic then. I'd accidentally written a well-structured book on my first attempt, but having to write a second book in such a short time span had proved to me that I didn't actually know how books were structured.

I didn't understand the skeletons that hold up books. I didn't know that they have skulls and spines and femurs and tibias, and without placing those bones in the correct places, they wouldn't be able to stand up as solid things of beauty. It wasn't formula—that word makes structure sound cheap and simple. It was essentialism. Story *needs* structure in order to *be* story.

I sat at that table and ignored the ocean outside the window. I cried a little and gritted my teeth more. I didn't learn how to write a book that weekend. That took a lot more time and much more practice (though I did eventually save that book, and I'm proud of it now).

But now I see that structure everywhere, and it's so beautiful. It will make your book feel strong, and right, and complete. If you ignore story structure, you risk pissing off your reader, who will *not* be able to articulate what they want from you—they'll just know you didn't provide it.

Let's avoid that.

We've already talked about your character arc in this memoir. You are the hero of this story (but this kind of hero doesn't normally wear a cape). You have to show your big personal change, or the reader will ask what was the point of reading your story.

You map that change onto a narrative arc, or story structure.

You *could* write all the scenes of your memoir and move them around until they feel right. This is definitely an option, and because you're already an accidental expert in story structure (as all consumers of Western media are), you'll know when you get it right. Many professional writers do exactly this. But it might take years to find that shape.

So let's shorten that cycle.

The Four-Act Structure

What! I don't even understand the three-act structure yet!

Don't worry! I love the four-act structure, as laid out by Larry Brooks in *Story Engineering*, but it's exactly the same as the three-act structure, only it's *understandable*. That noodly, wiggly middle act in the three-act structure, the big act, the act that everyone has a problem with filling is just broken up into two pieces, that's all. (I'll lay out some of his teachings here, in explaining the way that I use them, but I strongly recommend his book for more excellent information.)

Think of this story structure as four boxes.

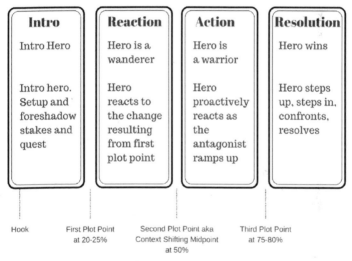

Intro	Reaction	Action	Resolution
Intro Hero	Hero is a wanderer	Hero is a warrior	Hero wins
Intro hero. Setup and foreshadow stakes and quest	Hero reacts to the change resulting from first plot point	Hero proactively reacts as the antagonist ramps up	Hero steps up, steps in, confronts, resolves

Hook   First Plot Point at 20-25%   Second Plot Point aka Context Shifting Midpoint at 50%   Third Plot Point at 75-80%

4-Act Structure, adapted from Larry Brooks

In the first box, you introduce yourself. You set up the stakes of your story. You gain the reader's empathy. Something happens (the hook) at the very beginning that grabs our attention because it's interesting and immediate, but it's not the first plot point (the first time things really change in the story). Your hook can be simple. All it has to do is make the reader interested enough to keep reading.

Then, *whap!* Now comes your first plot point. Something big happens, forcing change, and we move into the next phase of the story.

In the second box, you are *reacting* to the events and people around you. You're running, hiding, moving, avoiding—basically you're doing everything but attempting to make an honest, real change.

Bam! Another something happens, but this something is even bigger. It's big enough to make you reevaluate your own story. This is the context-shifting midpoint.

In the third box, because of that something happening, you turn into the person who *acts*, instead of the one who reacts. You're making changes, you're fighting, you're hitting, you're working to help yourself and perhaps those around you. But then—

BOOM! The worst thing happens. This is the dark moment of the soul, the time when things look the bleakest.

In the fourth box, you fight so hard that you finally triumph. You become the self you've been trying to change into, and in the process, you've fixed the external problem, too.

Each of these boxes is approximately 25 percent of the length of the total book. (Sometimes the first quarter and the last quarter are a little shorter than that, giving you a bit more room in the second and third quarters.)

The hero (that's you) has a different job in each box.

Sitting between the boxes are Big Things that Happen.

There. That's all it is. Four boxes: Introduction, Reaction, Action, Resolution.

Let's look at each one a little more closely, with a fictional example to go along with it.

Martina's Story

Martina would like to write a memoir about her marriage. Her big personal change is how she moved from being too timid to stand up for herself to becoming a fierce warrior, getting herself and her child out of an abusive relationship.

The first box: Here Martina will set up the stakes. She'll show us a scene or two from inside the marriage, the way she was then.

IMPORTANT: This is a story of abuse, but the worst thing Martina can do in this first box is start with a scene of her husband beating her.

Why?

If I come up to you on the street as a stranger and say, "My mother just died," you'll frown and say, "I'm sorry." But your heart won't be very moved. You'll likely be annoyed if I grab your arm and start to tell you everything about my mother. I'm a stranger to you.

But if your childhood best friend calls you and says her mother just died, you'll cry. You were practically raised in Mrs. Bailey's kitchen. You know what she meant to your friend—that they talked every single day and your friend made the two-hour drive to see her twice a week. You can understand your friend's pain, and you hurt for her.

You care, because you're invested. You're familiar with the stakes, and you have true empathy.

In the first box, during that first 20-25 percent of the

book, you set up the stakes. You introduce yourself and what matters to this story.

Perhaps our fictional and rather cliché-tastic Martina uses this space to tell the story of how she and Dennis met. They set up their first tiny apartment together. Dennis works overtime when Martina is pregnant and loses her job. The baby comes. Even if Dennis is sometimes short-tempered and yells a little too loudly, making the baby cry, he's wonderful with little Jasper. He bonds with the baby in a way Martina finds beautiful. Her own father was never around, and she'll do anything to make this family the strong, loving circle she never felt growing up. Martina chooses to show us the baby's first Christmas when Dennis worked so many hours that dark circles started forming under his eyes, but he desperately wanted to give Jasper an outdoor playset. He spends all night putting together the slide and the jungle gym that Jasper is still too young for. Martina's heart is full.

Then Jasper falls off the slide. Dennis is furious at Martina for not watching him well enough. For the first time, he slaps her.

This first plot point happens about 20 percent of the way through the book. We care enough about Martina to turn the page, to see how she'll react to this.

And react she does. In box two, she is the reactor. She chronicles how she and Dennis go to counseling. She's always said she wouldn't stay with a man who hit her even once, but Dennis is different. This was an accident, really. He would never do anything like that again. Even when, in this box, he scares her several times and slaps her twice more, she is *reacting*. She's telling herself it will be okay. She's hiding the evidence from friends. Larry Brooks says, "The goal could be survival, finding love, getting away from love gone bad, acquiring wealth, healing, attaining justice, stopping or catching the bad guys, preventing disaster, escaping danger, saving someone, saving the entire world, or anything else from the realm of human experience and dreams. But whatever the hero needs, there must be something opposing the hero's quest to achieve it. No opposition, no story." [17]

Then, right at the halfway mark, Dennis pushes her to the ground. She hits the kitchen island as she falls, breaking her arm. Jasper sees this happen. At three years old, he's old enough to remember this later.

This, my friends, is the context-shifting midpoint. When this happens, our hero (Martina in this case, *you* in your memoir) experiences something large that changes her into a person willing to fight.

[Pro tip: this midpoint shift is often death. If someone needs to die in your memoir, see if this placement works for you.]

Now we're in box three. Martina is now fighting for her son, to get him away from a father she knows will someday hurt him. She's scrounging money to get a lawyer and a new place to live. She's asking friends for help. She gets a job in secret, something she can do at home and keep hidden from Dennis. At every turn, she might be stymied, but she's still trying. She's acting, not just reacting.

And *BOOM!* (You knew this was coming, didn't you? That's the point! You *knew* this was coming! It wouldn't be satisfying without this dark moment of the soul.) Dennis gets drunk one night and hits Martina so hard her nose breaks. The seven-year-old Jasper watches, but instead of hiding like he normally does, he flies at his father to protect his mother. Dennis shakes him so hard Jasper bites his tongue. Dennis says that no matter where they go, he'll always find them, that they're his. Martina sees the blood pouring from her son's mouth and knows she's failed. They'll never get away.

But after that dark night of the soul, we enter the fourth box, the resolution box. We watch as Martina wakes up the next morning, both eyes blackened. She waits until Dennis goes to work, and she pulls out the secret suitcase she bought with her secret job earnings. She packs some changes of clothes and Jasper's Legos. She goes to the police station where she reports her injuries. They take her and Jasper to the local women's shelter. We jump forward in time a bit to see Martina living in her own small apartment, taking care of herself and her son. She's learned the tools to keep herself safe, and Dennis is in counseling and can only see Jasper on court-supervised visits. Martina will be okay, and so will Jasper, and that's all that matters.

This example worked well and simply because I was making it up. I got to make all the things work within their boxes, sliding them around easily, not constrained by truth. I knew what I was going for.

So imagine for a moment that in box three, when Martina was getting ready to leave him, that she just does. No major incident with Dennis occurs, she just gets an apartment and moves out and all is well forever.

That might be exactly what happened.

But writing it like that will let your reader down. Your reader won't know *why* she feels like it wasn't the best book she ever read, but she'll feel it.

That dark moment at the 75-80 percent mark is crucial, just as the context-shifting midpoint and the first plot point are. All these moments are needed.

Luckily, you can write them using what you already have in your outline.

Let's go back to Martina—say that her story really did go as I mentioned just above. She gets married, he hits her, she reacts but makes no real forward motion, he breaks her arm (Martina thought this was the midpoint), and she leaves.

As Martina's teacher, I know that if she uses the breaking of her arm as the book's midpoint but has no darker moment at the

75 percent mark, that the structure of her story will fail, disappointing the reader.

I ask, "What's the worst moment you had in that situation? Was it the broken arm? If so, can you move events around and fill in the spaces with new scenes so that the broken arm is your dark moment at the seventy-five percent mark?"

Martina says, "No, that *wasn't* my darkest moment. My darkest moment was one night when I watched Jasper slap a mosquito on his arm the same way his father slapped me. I can't write that as my dark moment, though. It's too quiet, isn't it?"

Nosirree! A quiet moment of revelation in which something internally shifts can be any of these moments: the first plot point, the midpoint, or the dark moment. Those quiet moments can be very powerful, in fact.

Exercise:

So now your job is this: go through your outline with the four-act structure in mind. Don't forget: you must show your big personal change in your memoir.

What three large (or quietly large) things got you to that change? Can you make those the first plot point? The midpoint? The dark moment? Can you move things around so you ease into the story, showing us in your life before things start to change? Can you draw the four boxes (introduction, reaction, action, resolution) around your scenes? If not, can you flip scenes around? Remember, you don't have to write chronologically if it works better for you not to.

You might not figure this out in one sitting. This is probably one of the most confusing tasks that I'm going to ask you to do. It's hard to get outside of yourself and look at your life from this bird's-eye point of view. If you have someone *firmly* inside your circle of trust, consider asking them to help you with it (bonus: if you explain four-act structure to them, you'll learn it better). This is a great place to use other writer friends if you're hooked into a community, too. You aren't sharing your actual work with them, remember. But asking structure questions and bouncing ideas against other people can help.

Take your time with this. Think about it while you're walking or in the shower. Take a bath and consider it, and be gentle with yourself.

But do try to keep this thinking time to a week or less. Don't let this step extend into a procrastination tool. It's okay to start your memoir with only a vague idea as to how this will work for you. It will come.

Chapter Twelve

DO I REALLY HAVE TO?

I just want to tell my story. Is that so wrong? Do I really have to think about this crap?

Yes, this stuff is hard. Like I said, structuring your memoir is one of the hardest things to do when working in this genre. This is where my students struggle the most.

And yes, you may have to chop huge ideas out of your outline. They might be great ideas! You may desperately want to write them! But you'll have to decide whether they fit *this* memoir. You might have to add things you never thought you'd need into it. Be okay with that change. It might look nothing like it did when you started.

Before you whine again in my general direction, I honestly believe giving your memoir a structure is necessary. Without it, your reader will be dissatisfied.

Unless the only reader you ever plan on having is yourself, you *have* to consider your audience.

And yes, those percentage marks that make you roll your eyes are crucial, too. It's literary gravity, an expected force. As you read both memoir and fiction going forward, note what happens at the halfway mark. You'll get to a point where you'll read something and identify it as that context-shifting midpoint, and you'll tilt the book to see you're right in the middle of the spine, or you'll glance down at the percentage mark in your Kindle to see 48-52 percent. I had a student once say that surely *The Glass Castle* didn't follow this formula. I brought in my print copy with Post-it notes wrapped around the first plot point, the midpoint, and the dark moment, each separated by exactly 25 percent of the book. Now, there's a chance Jeannette Walls didn't think consciously about this when she was writing, but she was enough of a storyteller that this just felt right when she revised. (Bam! Teacher: 1, Student: 100 because I *really* adore my students, even when they're wrong.)

A popular metaphor is that story structure is like sex: there's foreplay, the sex itself, climax, and recovery. A different order *can* exist, sure, but it's more satisfying in the order we naturally desire as human beings.

And now that you know about this structure (story structure, that is—you're probably well aware of the way sex works), you'll see it everywhere. You'll see it in the shows you watch on Netflix and in the newest Star Wars movie. You'll see it in short stories and over the course of five-book sagas. There's a strong chance you'll be annoyed by my having shared this with you—I know I sure was when I finally saw the structure all around me. How could I not have noticed before? How did everyone know about it before I did?

Pro tip: Everyone who talks about story structure is saying the same thing, whether it's Blake Snyder's *Save the Cat*, the three-act *Story Grid,* Larry Brooks's four-act structure, or any of a host of others. The same design is in play, even if all the words we use to talk about it are different. This made me batty for years. I'd finally get the hang of one of them (*Save the Cat*, for instance) and then I'd come across someone else's ideas. As I'm perpetually looking for the magic bullet (aren't we all?), I'd dive into this new method. *Wait,* I'd think. *Is this thing he's calling a Plot Point actually a Catalyst? Is a pinch point the same thing as Bad Guys Close In?*

Forget the names. Use the ones I list here or make up new words for yourself. I personally resonate strongly with the Larry Brooks's structure, and if you like the way I talked about the four boxes above, it might work for you, too. But the real power is in knowing that there *is* a structure to story, and that readers need it to feel satisfied.

You can absolutely have as your goal to piss off all readers—being controversial can increase attention. But for God's sake, don't do it by accident merely because you haven't learned the rules.

Chapter Thirteen

WRITING THE DAMN BOOK

Yes! It's finally time!

And look. I have every single bit of confidence in you. I've had many students gaze at me with the same deer-in-the-headlights expression that you're giving me now, and they finished their memoirs even though they never thought they could.

You're going to, also.

Make that decision right now. This isn't an "I hope I can do this" situation. This is an "I'm going to write and *finish* my memoir" state of affairs.

You're going to do this.

The next question I always get is "*How* the frak am I supposed to do this?"

You're going to write this book scene by scene. That's all.

Each of the scenes in your book will fit into one of those four structural boxes we talked about.

But you might not actually know where those scenes fit yet. That's okay.

You do *not* have to write in chronological order. You can write scenes from your outline in any order at all. Write what excites you. If you can't wait to write that summer vacation morning memory, write it now. Move toward what you *want* to write. You don't have to start at the beginning. You can write scenes and throw them into a virtual bin in the middle of the floor and sort them into their appropriate boxes later. You'll be able to look at each scene and ask yourself, "was I reacting at this point? Or was I the actor in my own life, making my own decisions? Does this particular bit belong in Act Two or Act Three?" But you decide those things later. For now, you're just writing a crappy first draft that you can fix later. If you winced at that, start trying to accept crappiness. Personally, I find it useful to challenge myself to write *truly* terribly. At least then I have a goal I can strive for, and it works—I get my words done, and they're always, always fixable. Yours will be, too.

However, many people (including myself) are linear writers and don't want to write out of order. We like to start at the beginning and write through to the end. That's fine, too, just know that you don't have to stick to it. I get pretty rigid myself, both in fiction and memoir, and I shove myself through scenes like I'm trying to fit a jar of peanut butter into a thimble. *I will get there if it kills me.* This can be unpleasant, but it's my way. You'll find your way as you go.

Here's a bit of advice to help you get there.

THE BEGINNING

1. Have a word-count goal and write it on your calendar for the week. Don't write out your word count goal for the whole book, because I guarantee you'll miss a week's goal, and then you'll have to rejigger your whole calendar for a month or more (ask me how I know). But if you have three hours free for writing this week, and if you think you can get three thousand words written in that time, plan it. On Sunday morning, you'll write a thousand. Tuesday night, five hundred. Thursday, another five hundred. Friday morning, the last thousand. Write it down, then when the time rolls around, *write*.

2. Celebrate that first day of writing! You will feel elated, guaranteed. Huzzah! You did it! You've started something *huge!* If you drink, have a glass of champagne. If you don't, eat your favorite dessert. Toast yourself and your supreme daring. You're amazing! You're a writer! (You're a writer if you're writing. That's how it works. Claim that.)

3. Know that the next time you sit down, it *might* not feel as great as it did the first day. The high does wear off, and writing becomes more painful the further we go into a piece of work. That's okay, and it's totally normal. I often liken it to exercise (gah)—it sucks to work out, but it always feels good later.

4. Your voice is your voice is your voice. You'll have days when you *know* in your very bones that you're the very worst writer who ever lived. A caveman scratching symbols on a wall in charcoal is a better writer than you are. And then you'll have days when your writing is miraculous. Your words could convert a Catholic nun to Satanism. Your sentences leap off the page and build castles around your ears. The astonishing thing is this: when you go back to revise (later!), you won't be able to tell which were the days you wrote "well" or "badly." Your voice is your voice. The way we feel about our writing changes just like our moods. Don't trust your moods. Just keep showing up, day after day.

5. After you've begun, it's normal to feel that you'll never finish. It's such a herculean effort just to write one scene, how are you ever going to write the whole book? It's an impossible task. You can't do this.

Yes, you can.

Yes, you will.

One scene at a time. Or even just one paragraph at a time. Many short writing sessions add up to a finished book. You're on the way.

THE MIDDLE

1. The middle part might be difficult. Wait. It *will* be. Often called "the sagging middle," this is common. I call a first draft the "who cares" draft because it's easy, when stuck in the middle, to think that nobody cares. Your mom doesn't care. Your husband is sick of hearing about it. Your kids roll their eyes.

Worst of all, *you* stop caring.

It's hard work. Who's going to want to read all this crap? No one, that's who. Might as well quit before I waste any more time on this stupid endeavor.

Normal! That's so, so normal. No one cares, not even you.

That changes—you'll just have to trust me on this. You'll find your mojo again, and when you're revising (later!), you'll *love* the book again. Accept that you might not love it while writing it.

2. Find software that helps you stay organized. I recommend Scrivener as a word processing program and all-around excellent writer's toolbox. Microsoft Word is a powerful if sometimes aggravating tool, and you can certainly use it for a whole book. Many, many writers do, and all of the publishing industry relies on it every step of the way through submissions and edits.

But Scrivener has an excellent feature that's missing from Word, and I consider it an essential feature for memoirists. It holds each scene/chapter in a separate bucket. This means you can write your scenes in any order, and then just drag and drop them where you want them to be. Later, when you send your book to your editor or your agent (more on this in a future chapter), you'll export your book as a complete, tidy Word document, but while you're actually writing, you can dart in and out of the different buckets.

Also, Scrivener is great at holding other things in other buckets—research, photos, web pages, lists of characters, etc. I'm writing in it right now. I even use it to organize my classes. It's an organization tool that just *works* for writers. At the time of writing, it's $45 USD, and worth every penny. (Here are my affiliate links, if you'd like to explore it: Mac or Windows.)

THE END

1. Don't let the ending intimidate you. *I'm scared of writing the ending. I want to get it right.*

Of course you are! The end is scary! You've spent all this time writing your book—what if you screw it up at the last minute?

This is how we get over this, and this is what I have everyone in my classes do: **write the ending right after you write your beginning.**

Even if you're a linear writer, do this exercise (don't worry—it will change in revision. This is just a rough draft) right after you've written your first scene.

2. Catch the change. Remember that in your memoir, you are chronicling the change in yourself that occurred over the course of time. The ending will show the synthesis of that. If you're writing about the three years you spent teaching English in China, and if your Big Personal Change was that you moved from being scared of everything to being brave, then in that last chapter, your reader wants to see that. Tell us about it. Show us in detail how you landed back in the States. Your mother wanted to meet you at the airport, but you told her no, you'd grab a cab. You walk into her house a different person. Show us that.

3. You already know the ending. It's probably the most recent thing to happen to you in your whole memoir, anyway. It will be easy to write.

So write it now.

Then you'll have your ending, a pushpin on the map to show where you're heading. You'll spend the rest of your time in the book driving in the direction of this ending, and knowing your ending informs the rest of your writing.

Of course, it can change! You might write the end of your book only to figure out that it's actually where you want to start (this happens more often than you'd think). Perhaps it gives you an idea for a different structure of your book. Do you want to start your book with the you of today and then flash back? Do you want to anchor the beginning in the present instead of the past?

Don't worry too much about the answers. They'll change, and that's normal.

Don't worry, either, about putting things in their rightful places now. The chapter you think comes first may later turn out to be your fifth chapter. Things change as you go, and inspiration comes while you're writing. You can't sit down and just determine the best shape of your book because your book wants to tell the shape to you as you go.

Just write.

Start now. Take it day by day, in small steps.

Aim for your word count.

Don't stop until you're done.

You've got this.

Chapter Fourteen

HOW TO GET OUT OF YOUR OWN WAY AND WRITE

Just write, you say? How am I supposed to do that?

Welcome to the part of the book that's the most exciting to many! You may have skipped story structure and flipped right to this chapter. That's fine. But go back and read that section eventually, or a plague of sea monsters will head straight for your house through the sewers. Just a little spell I set up. You *need* to read about story structure.

But since you're here (or if you got here the right way, you darling teacher's pets, you), let's dive in.

Getting the Writing Done

Actually getting the words onto the page is so much harder than it sounds, isn't it?

That's normal.

You're normal.

Once, I was teaching this class at Stanford, and we were worry-busting. We were about six weeks in. The honeymoon was over. The students had each already turned in more than ten thousand words to me by that point. It wasn't a distant dream—at this point, every single one of them was in the trenches, up to their knees in muddy, swampy words that weren't acting the way they wanted them to.

"Worry-busting! Who's first?"

Tina raised her hand. "I'm worried that I just can't do this."

I adjusted my glasses. "Okay. Why?"

"Because it's so hard. I hate doing it." She kept her gaze on her notebook, and her voice got tight. "I just think that I might not... I might not be a real writer."

I laughed.

Tina looked up sharply. The class held its collective breath. Was I *laughing* at her?

"Tina!" I said. "Don't you know what that means?"

She shook her head, her eyes wide.

I looked around the class. "How many of you think that real writers enjoy writing?"

Almost all their hands went up.

"Oh, no, no, no!" I grinned. "Writers *hate* writing. Tina, guess what?"

She shook her head again, though I could see she was starting to get it.

I said, "You're a real writer."

Tina's smile widened.

"Anyone else in here hate writing?"

Almost all the hands went up again.

"Good! You're all real writers!"

There's a myth that we get from all parts of media (but most specifically from the first scene in *Romancing the Stone*) that says that writing is ecstasy. As writers, we're thought to leave our bodies, our fingers dancing over the keyboard, "taking dictation" from the muse.

Hell, no.

If you wait for the muse to write, she'll go on permanent strike. I *hate* the fiction of the muse. It's debilitating to so many writers who wait to be struck by the right bolt of lightning, the one that will send them to the page with gorgeous prose or perfect poetry flowing from their fingertips. What they don't know is that she's not coming. Their muse, knowing she wouldn't be needed, jumped a bus to Vegas and is right now chain-smoking cigarettes and betting on nickel machines in the Bellagio.

Your muse only shows up when you do.

That's the only time. As W. Somerset Maugham said, "I write only when inspiration strikes. Fortunately, it strikes every morning at nine o'clock sharp."

Writing *is* the muse. Ideas pretty much only come to me when I'm in the physical act of writing. My muse is just blue-collar Rachael. I show up at the desk. I open the document. I start typing. After a little while, my muse comes into the office, reeking of smoke and cheap brandy, but she sits on the couch and starts to feed me ideas.

The muse comes from doing work.

(Okay, I guess I don't hate the idea of the muse—I just hate how she's prayed for as if she's the one who's going to turn on the tap. No, *you* do that. She shows up later to clap you on the back while trying to take all the credit.)

As Nora Roberts says, "Sister Mary Responsibility kicks the muse's ass every time." And Sister Mary Responsibility wants you to work this shit out for yourself. So let's get cracking.

1. Finding Time

In my mind, the best way to write would be to find a whole day—or better yet, a whack of days—during which I could lock myself in a hotel room overlooking the ocean and write the better part of a book.

Of course, this doesn't work. The time never comes (and ocean-view hotel rooms are expensive, y'all!). I spent, oh, seven years or so trying to find the perfect block of time, convinced it was always coming up in the next few weeks.

I was procrastinating. Of course, I was.

So, how do you *fix* procrastination?

I honestly don't know the complete answer, but I know what works for me.

First of all, according to *AsapSCIENCE*'s Mitchell Moffi, "Human motivation is highly influenced by how imminent the reward is perceived to be. The further away the reward is, the more you discount its value. This is often referred to as present bias, or hyperbolic discounting." [18]

Present bias means doing hard work isn't as pleasurable as doing something else in this moment. (Duh. Writing is hard. Therefore, we prefer to do something easier in the now-moment, like passively scrolling Facebook.) The further away the reward or deadline, the easier it is to push work (even if it's enjoyable) aside.

And why is this?

The findings show that we think of our future selves the same way we do a person we have never met.

This is huge.

The Rachael of the future, the one who has a deadline in three weeks, would probably really appreciate it if Rachael of today did a bit more extra writing.

But I don't *know* that Rachael.

In my brain, and in yours, when we push something off to another day, we are expecting *someone we don't know* to pick up the slack later.

It explains why I've never been able to figure out why I'm such a jerk to myself. *Why* did I leave this article for the last day? Why would I do that to myself if I'm supposed to love myself, which, for the most part, I do?

The answer: I do it to someone else. When I procrastinate, it doesn't feel like it's hurting future Rachael. I'm hurting someone who doesn't really exist to me.

When you put off writing your memoir, you're relegating it to someone you don't know, someone who might be better at it than you are. Then, of course, the next day comes around, and surprise! You're still not ready to begin it.

This is why it always feels like a shock. We do it to ourselves because we're not empathizing with the stranger we've relegated the task to.

So give that person (future you) a little empathy. Do a little work for her sake, every day.

And yes, I'm a big believer in little bits of time that add up to finished work, and I'm just as big a believer in routine. If you get in the habit of waking up just twenty minutes earlier than usual so you can catch five hundred words before getting in the shower, the muse will start to show up at the same time every morning. The muse *loves* routine. She's a woman who appreciates a good Excel spreadsheet. When she's not in Vegas.

So look at your calendar.

First, block off your relaxation/play times. Yes, before your writing time. This genius tip is from Jessica Abel, whose book *Growing Gills* is excellent. I constantly try to slither out of my writing time because I feel like I haven't had enough time to lie around and read or watch TV or play with the dogs. But if I schedule that time first, it makes setting aside my writing time so much easier.

After you schedule recreational time around work and other life obligations, *then* schedule regular writing time.

Aim for forty-five minutes a day, five days a week. Fit it in somewhere. Or less if you don't have that much. More if you do. Build up from your base.

During that time you've scheduled, just sit in your chair and try to work. That's all. You just have to show up and be willing to type.

I *do* have a few other tricks up my sleeve to help with this.

2. Get Out

I've been writing for years, so now I can do it in my own house. As I type this, my feet are up on my roll top desk, my computer perched on top of a small dog resting in my lap. But for most of my professional writing career, I've needed to leave the house to write. This is most especially true for first drafts of fiction. I *still* can't pull this off at home.

Home, to me, means a thousand square feet of Things I Should Be Doing. This morning, while on breaks from writing, I've washed a load of clothes, hung out hand-knit socks to dry, done the dishes, started another load of laundry, let the dogs in and out approximately four hundred times, and made myself two snacks. It's not even noon.

But when I leave the house and go somewhere else, laptop in hand? I've got nothing to do but write. I'm alone in the cafe or the library. I pull out my computer. I open the lid.

I'm all set to go, no distractions.

OH, NO, what is that shiny ribbon of internet highway that gleams before me?

3. Freedom

Buy this program (freedom.to), or something like it. This is a $2.50/month program for the Mac and PC that kicks you physically off the internet. You tell it how long to go offline, then you type in your password, and you're locked out. The only way to get back in is to actually shut down your entire computer and reboot (which I've done once or twice).

So I get to the cafe, grab my coffee, and allow myself to check email while I eat my carrot muffin. Then *without thinking* or arguing with myself, I hit Freedom and enter forty-five minutes.

Bam. I have nothing else to do but work. Even if I would prefer to die of boredom, I eventually get around to writing some words. And if, while I'm working, I think of something that I must look up on the internet, I jot it down, thus clearing it from my brain.

After forty-five minutes, the computer bonks and, *DING DING DING*, tweets and email messages fall from the sky like confetti. I give myself fifteen minutes to screw around.

Then I do it all over again.

This idea of forty-five/fifteen-minute work cycles is popular among writers—forty-five minutes seems to be a perfect amount of brain-power time. It's an extension of the Pomodoro Technique, which encourages you to work in thirty minutes work cycles with five minutes off. I've never cared for the Pomodoro schedule, because I can't handle a five-minute break. That isn't enough for me to both pee *and* get another snack *and* check email.

If Freedom is too expensive, get a different app. There are many. But get one. It will save your writing life.

4. Write or Die

More than once, this has been misheard when I say it out loud.

(Okay, maybe I mumble.) "Writer, die? Is that an order?" ask my confused students.

Fear not. (Well, fear a little bit.) Write or Die is a word processing app. That's all it is. It costs $20 at the time of writing (I'm not an affiliate; I just love the product) and I would pay ten times that for it if I had to.

What does it do?

It's a place for you to write. It is *not* a place to store your work. When you finish writing, you have to copy and paste your work into whatever application you normally use, usually Word or Scrivener.

So what's special about it?

It reinforces you to write, in a couple of very concrete ways (some good! Some bad!).

When you open Write or Die, you tell it how much time you'd like to write, and you tell it how many words you want to get. This, delightfully, gives you a words-per-hour to aim for, which is something I like because I'm a Woman Who Likes Her Goals.

The thing is, when we're writing, we often space out. We do this is because writing is hard, and people—as mentioned—don't like doing hard things. The other day I found myself completely revamping my entire budgeting system just to avoid writing. Doing that was easier, so I spent hours importing Excel files.

And it's just so *easy* to drift off while writing. One second I'm in the story, the next I'm staring out the window wondering if that really, truly was Chris Hemsworth's body in *Thor: Ragnarok* or was he enhanced, CGI-wise? If so, how much? (Now you're wondering, too. Let's all take a moment.)

So, your mind wanders. Time passes. Without a paid tutor standing over you, watching your fingers and rapping them with a ruler when you stop writing, no one will notice the time passing, least of all you.

Enter Write or Die.

In the level of the app I use, when I stop writing, the screen goes red after twenty seconds of no keyboard activity. That's all. It goes from white to pale pink to red to bright red. This catches my eye and reminds me that I'm supposed to be writing, not spacing out. It's all I need. I've used it in this mode for almost ten years, and I'll probably never change the settings to make them more alarming.

But if you're more of a masochist?

In addition to the screen going red, you can set it to make rude noises. If you stop writing, suddenly your computer starts screaming at you—car alarms and babies crying and, most distressingly, Milli Vanilli songs. To make that stop, you'll type anything.

And that's the secret, you know. Typing anything. Getting the crappiest words down so that you can fix them later. That's all that matters in this gig.

If you set the program one notch harder, it'll start to drop gigantic spiders (or office horrors or Grumpy Cat, which really seems like more of a reward to me) onto your screen while it's glowing fiery red and babies are howling like they've been left on the snowy moors.

On the craziest setting?

Are you ready for this?

Seriously. Make sure you're sitting down.

On the hardest setting, after you haven't been typing during your grace period, **IT ERASES YOUR WORDS.**

You don't get them back.

Control-Z doesn't work. Your words leave, erasing backward, and they don't stop disappearing till you type again.

Believe me, if this doesn't get you typing again, then you should take the rest of the day off and maybe call a priest because you might be dying. (My friend Adrienne always says, "It's not called Write or Annoy. It's called Write or Die for a *reason*!")

Lovely little program that it is, it also gives you rewards if you'd like them. Your computer can purr when you hit your goal, or a puppy in a birthday hat can show up with a triumphant blare of happy trumpets. You can set a custom image to show when you hit your word count.

(Aside—I can imagine some people use *shocking* custom images as a reward. Completely unrelated, I need a screenshot of Chris Hemsworth's chest, stat.)

I love Write or Die so much I've put it into the acknowledgments of at least two of my novels. Once I wrote an entire novel that came to me under such difficult circumstances, I could only manage to write words while using Write or Die for fifteen minutes at a time. I couldn't write any of my first drafts without it. Every time I think that I'm a failure, that *this* is finally the point at which I won't be able to produce words, I remember that Write or Die exists, fire it up, and draft some atrocious writing.

Then I fix the writing, and I do my happy-writer dance, which looks suspiciously like my chocolate-peanut-butter-ice-cream dance. Go get the program.

5. Music

For me, most books have a soundtrack. I listen to music on my phone since my computer is offline while I work. Whatever media player you use, the key is this: **use the music as a way to drop right back into the writing.** Don't end up procrastinating (I see you over there!) by making the perfect playlist. Drop three or five albums that you think might work into a list, hit shuffle, and start writing. When a song doesn't work? Hit skip and when you're done writing, throw it off the list. Later, when you hear a song on the radio that would be perfect for the list, add it then. Your playlist grows organically that way, and when the book is close to being done, the list will be pretty much perfect.

Music also helps you create the routine that lures the muse

out from behind the couch where she's currently hiding. I have a local radio station that plays only songs from the 1920s and '30s. I only listen to it while I'm driving to the library where I write. I don't actively make myself think about my work while I'm driving —I prefer to let my subconscious take care of a lot of the thinking—but the sound of the songs primes me in a Pavlovian way to write. I only noticed this when, on a drive where I was *not* on my way to write and had accidentally left the station selected, I could feel my brain gearing up to write. It was gathering itself, getting ready. I know that sounds odd, and it's hard to explain, but I could feel my attention shift inward, the way I focus when I'm writing. It was a revelation.

A bonus to having a writing soundtrack is that whenever you hear that Moby or Sigur Rós song five or ten years from now, it will *still* bring you back to the moment of writing this book. There's one song in particular that I once put on repeat while writing a death scene, and it can still sometimes make me cry to hear it.

No music for you? Some people can't listen to words (I can't, so I love movie soundtracks) and others can't listen to music at all. I recommend the White Noise app (available for free for Android and iPhone at the time of writing). If you put it on the pink noise setting, it's ideal for cafes. Pink noise is a color (frequency) of sound that actually works to mask the human voice, so while you can hear people talking, it's harder to pick out their actual words, keeping your own words safe from distraction.

6. Just Do It

Writers write. I completely, totally understand wanting with all your heart to write and not writing, because I did that for so many years. It's *such* a frustrating feeling. But the only way to get the urge out of your system and feel satisfied is to do the work, even when it's shitty work (and it will be, at first. All first drafts will be shitty, even from pro writers. I keep mentioning this because, even though it's the law, it's easy to forget). Just sit your butt down in the chair and do it, a little at a time. Keep writing and revision separate. There will be time to fix the terrible draft later.

Pro tip: Again, if you say *I can't write this way because I have to make everything perfect before I move on,* that's fine ONLY if this method works for you AND you're completing full books. In other words, if you're completing what you set out to complete, then yay! But if you want to write your memoir but are stymied because of the whole "perfection" thing, then you need to barrel through a really horrible first draft. Your method isn't working. Try a new one, friend. Try this one.

Chapter Fifteen

SELF-CARE

Trauma

If remembering past events feels difficult, that's because it really can be pretty terrifying and triggering.

Our brains, when presented with concrete evidence of the past, can sometimes feel again like we're back there. When we write down our stories, we're building that concrete, visible, re-readable evidence.

Keith Oatley (emeritus professor of cognitive psychology, University of Toronto) says that reading produces a vivid simulation of reality, one that "runs on minds of readers just as computer simulations run on computers." [19]

What this means is that our brains believe the tale we tell them, as if we're reliving the moment. Scientists have long understood the established areas of the brain involved in language processing: Broca's area and Wernicke's area. But in 2006, a study [20] found that words with strong odor associations (like "lavender" or "cinnamon") lit up a reader's olfactory cortex. Words like "velvet" and "leathery" lit up the sensory cortex. Words like "kick" and "grab" lit up the motor cortex.

So if you read a story about a person getting onto a bike, your brain prepares your actual muscles to ride that bike. The lizard brain in the back of our mind is ready to smell coffee if we read the word. That same lizard brain is the one that makes you scream and cover your face while watching a horror movie on the couch, even though you know the leaping zombie can't get out of the television.

When you write your memoir, your logical brain knows you're safe, just like you know you're safe from Freddy Krueger.

That doesn't help, though, when your lizard brain is reading the words you wrote down and screaming *danger*.

It's okay.

Having flashbacks or a storm of weeping or even PTSD symptoms is common. During the exploration of her memories, one of my students remembered something she'd hidden deeply for years. When faced with this sudden revelation, she felt herself spiraling, and she didn't have a plan for self-care. She thought she'd been writing a lighthearted memoir about her crazy-fun family, not an exploration of buried sexual abuse.

I'm not saying this will happen to you. Not everyone has this dark and traumatic a past to trudge through. But many do.

Shame

Right up there with trauma, shame is something that can rise up from the ink on the page.

To this I say, good!

There's nothing like writing about your shame. *Your* shame. No one else's. Sure, feel free to mention the shame your mom felt about her body, or the shame your father had for not living up to his obligations.

But the most interesting part of your memoir is *your* shame.

Why? It's a universal emotion, and I personally believe it to be the most powerful one. It keeps families, generations, and even whole countries in bondage. We all understand its blackness—we've all felt the surface shame of saying the wrong thing at the wrong time, and we've all experienced the soul-deep shame of feeling we're the wrong person in the wrong body doing all the wrong things.

I mentioned Brené Brown earlier—as a world-renowned shame researcher, she's done studies that show that shame is universal. You can't avoid it. You not only have it in your past, but you will have it in your future, too. Recognizing it is crucial.

And the best news is this: there's a cure for shame. It's not a small cure; it doesn't cure some of it. It cures *all* of it.

Here's how Brown boils it down:

- Know what triggers your shame.
- Reality check those triggers.
- Reach out and share: speak it out loud.
- Talk to yourself like someone you love.
- Reach out to someone you love.
- Tell your story.

Brown says that secrets intensify shame, creating a perfect vicious circle. We feel shame, so we hide it away. That secret makes the shame worse. She says that shame needs three things to grow: secrecy, silence, and judgment.

The antidote, she says, is empathy. Shame can't survive empathy. [21]

You've felt that, right? When you finally confess to a loved one something that you thought they'd stop loving you for? And they look at you and say, "Oh, yeah. I've been there. That's so hard." This is why twelve-step meetings are so powerful. Even if you can't start by naming the shame to loved ones, you can share your shame with other people, relative strangers, who nonetheless completely understand you. They've been there, too.

So, if you can, I really believe in sharing your shame as much as you feel able to.

Methods of sharing shame:

Google "memoir writing group" or "memoir critique group." You can meet with a group either in person (check MeetUp) or online. Join a local memoir class at the closest community college or extension program. Make sure, of course, before you show or tell anyone anything, that it's a safe space. Make sure the teacher or group leader puts value on kind critique, not the harsh, harmful critique that some groups use. Email and ask them directly how it works.

Then jump off the metaphoric cliff.

Tell them your worst.

Your hands will shake. So will your voice. You will feel ill to the bone. I've seen it so many times, and it always looks the same. You will be *sure* the other writers will hate you, will be horrified, will be traumatized, will be angry with you for sharing something so taboo.

And you know what? This is what will happen: you'll get knowing looks. You'll get valuable writing advice. Most of all, you'll feel empathy flowing toward you.

And the shame will die. It might take many liberal applications of empathy, but it will happen.

Planning for Self-Care

I want you to plan for your self-care *before* you hit a rough patch.

Personally, I like to drive. I have a convertible SmartCar that I adore. I know that when I need self-care, I get in it and head west for the coast. I live in a place where I can see the San Francisco Bay every day from the hill where I walk my dogs, but it's harder to get to the ocean. It's a good hour's drive, at least, and it's never easy to find the time. But when I'm feeling super stressed by writing, I drive toward the coast. I listen to my favorite songs and sing at the top of my lungs. Sometimes I listen to podcasts, other times I let the stereo fall silent. When I get to the waves, I just watch them. I breathe.

When writing (or anything else) has me stressed out, I have a pretty long list of other things that help me take care of myself. Here are some, in case you want to crib some ideas:

- **A bath.** This is physical. It involves your actual body, your skin, all your senses. It gets you out of your head for a little while.
- **Yoga.** Same thing. I use my body to help quiet the mind.
- **Tea.** I brew my favorite decaf tea in my favorite wee, pale-blue teapot. (You can brew real, caffeinated tea! I'm just a lightweight when it comes to caffeine.)
- **Read**. I say screw the world, I'm going to read. I get in bed because, let's face it, there's nowhere better to read than under your own covers. Reading on the couch is nice. Reading in bed in the middle of the day? Heaven.
- **Making**. I make something with my hands. I knit, or spin wool, or bake bread. I draw, I calligraph something, I bumble around with my studio journal,

pasting in wishes and coloring the pages. I do something creative that *isn't* writing.

- **Friends.** I have my own circle of empathy, a group of people who will listen to me admit anything and still be ready to fight on my side. Cultivate this.
- **Nap.** Like reading in bed (and in my world, they're often connected!), napping during the middle of the day can be the most decadent, delicious gift to yourself.
- **Therapy.** Nothing better. I like to put myself back into therapy anytime I feel a need for it, which for me is about every five or seven years. This is the ultimate in self-care. Highly recommended.

I understand, of course, that you have a life. You have a job or two. You have kids. You can't find time for laundry, let alone writing, let alone a bath or a *nap*.

But keep this list in mind if you find your writing stressing you out. That's not something you can help, exactly. Writing about hard times *is* triggering for the writer, no matter how mentally healthy she is.

So know what tools you can use. Know what tools *don't* work for you. You'll notice I don't have working out on my list. Working out (besides walking and yoga) serves to stress me out, no matter how good it is for me. When I'm looking for self-care, I'm more of a massage and bath oil kind of girl.

Exercise:

Write *your* personal self-care list.

What goes on it?

What should you keep off?

Make a note of how to notice when you need it. It's okay to cry and write (it can be *great* to cry and write) but at what point will you back up and give yourself the gift of a break?

Who will give you empathy? Again, do *not* show your work to anyone who isn't in your writing group. As Brown says, "If we share our shame story with the wrong person, they can easily become one more piece of flying debris in an already dangerous storm." [22] But *do* feel emboldened to talk to a safe friend *about* what you're writing. "I can't show you my writing, but it's about the debt we're drowning in. I don't know if we'll ever get out. Can I talk to you about that?"

I know this sounds *so frightening*.

But taking care of yourself well might change your life. You can do it.

Chapter Sixteen

WRITING MEDITATION

I have a lot of tools in my writing toolbox. It's good to have a hammer. Everyone needs one of those. But if you're trying to saw a board, your hammer won't be much use.

The *most* useful tool in my writer's toolbox is meditation.

Whoops! Before you cart this book to the bonfire, I swear this is not woo-woo. It's scientific (brain scans show meditation improves mental focus). It's secular. No religion was harmed (or called upon) in the writing of this chapter.

The hardest thing about writing is the thinking, right? As a society, we're not used to thinking very hard about one thing for longer than sixty or eighty seconds at a time. When you sit down at the computer to write, or when you pull out your notebook and put pen to paper, one of the greatest challenges is to stay present, to catch those thoughts that dance as randomly as dust motes in sunlight.

Meditation is push-ups for the mind.

I mean it exactly like that.

Meditation makes the muscles in your mind stronger, more willing to work, less upset when distractions occur, and more ready to circle back and do a little more work before heading for another cup of coffee.

When I teach memoir (or fiction, for that matter), I give my students a three-minute meditation explanation. I'm giving you the even more abbreviated version here.

Three simple steps to secular meditation:

1. Sit (or lie down, I don't care—I do both, depending on how I feel). Strict Meditators (I am not one) will tell you not to lie down, lest you fall asleep. But I can barely sleep in a bed—wouldn't that be *nice*, if I happened to drop into a nap?

2. Think about your breath. I count to ten to keep myself thinking about it. When I'm suddenly at fourteen, I know I've spaced out. And what I mean by thinking about your breath is to just notice it. Every breath is a little bit different. You don't have to breathe deeply or in any certain way. Just watch how your lungs fill, or how your stomach rises, or feel how the air moves through your nose.

3. Get distracted.

Repeat steps 2 and 3.

That's it.

Start with five minutes a day. Move up to ten, gradually. No need to ever go higher, though you can if you like.

That's all it is. That third step, the distraction one, is the part that freaks people out, that makes them think they're bad at meditation. The fact is, they're not. *Your brain will get distracted.* If it doesn't, you're probably dead and you should have someone call 911 for you. My brain gets distracted on a split-second basis. This is not an exaggeration—sometimes I can only hold on to watching my breath for a half-second at a time. Yes, it's frustrating. Meditation is only this: learning to be okay with getting distracted, and gently going back to what you were trying to do (without beating yourself up).

Try a little now.

There! You've got a stronger mind! You may only be able to do a couple of push-ups at first, but if you meditate a tiny bit today, your brain gets stronger and happier (literally).

Where is this super useful?

Your writing practice. It's *directly* usable.

The next time you go back to the page, you'll write a sentence, you'll get distracted, and you'll be a little bit easier on yourself. Your brain is a little bit stronger, and at the same time, you're a bit gentler on yourself. You've done a few of those mental push-ups. Now you can jump right back into writing after wondering how on earth that cat got so fat when you know for a fact you don't feed him that much.

It can't hurt. It can only help. No time? You can do it before you fall asleep (this used to be the only time I could find to practice, and it made sleeping *so* much better).

Mental push-ups that lead to better sleep? Better writing? That I can do with my eyes closed? Why not?

Exercise:

You can use meditation to pull out *more* memories. Meditate for a while, as stated above, for maybe three to ten minutes. There are *so* many apps to help with this. I like Insight Timer. It has nice chimes.

Then, when you're ready, imagine a room in your past you'd like to revisit to look for memories.

For me, I choose my mother's bedroom.

I pick something I know I remember. *The water-bed with its puffed fabric headboard.*

Then, in my mind, I walk slowly around the room. What do I bump into that I'd forgotten until this moment? *The huge quilt frame Dad made for her.* What do I smell? *The powdery scent of Chloé perfume from her handkerchief drawer.*

Keep moving around the room. Once you stub your toe on a memory, play with it in your mind. At this point, let your brain get distracted. It's okay to follow your thoughts around. You might fly off to the underground Paris nightclub where you met the man who would become your husband. Walk around that room now. What was on the walls? Be okay with not being able to remember, but be open to being surprised by how much you can recall in this meditative state.

Chapter Seventeen

PRESERVE MEMORY MOVING FORWARD

This is a great place to nag you about keeping a journal. Yes, I'm aware you're already a little overwhelmed with the idea of all this writing—adding more to your list of writing to-dos isn't ideal.

I understand.

I'm one of those people who likes the idea of a journal much more than I like keeping one. You might be the same. I have dreamy images of myself either writing with a dip quill (I used to, in my early twenties, when I was young enough to get away such pretentiousness). The same mist-covered vision allows me to see myself at ninety-five, laughing softly at the wonderful things that happened in my long life as I turn the pages as brittle as the skin of the backs of my hands.

I've always loved diaries, or at least, the idea of them. One of the very first things I ever coveted was one of those pink locking diaries. Remember them? With the teeny tiny key, and all the promise it held? When you're seven, your parents have all the keys. You have a fraying teddy bear and a lot of confusion around the word "polite."

I knew, though, that if I had a key that opened a book that only I could write in... Well, then I'd finally have things to write!

I got the diary for Christmas. Hearing that small snick the key made in the lock made me delirious with joy.

I wrote across the top of the first page. *STAY OUT*. My handwriting was perfect, the lines thick and dark.

Second page: *THIS MEANS YOU.*

Third page. *I REALLY MEAN IT. DON'T READ THIS. I'LL GET YOU.*

I promptly ran out of things to write.

Every evening, I'd unlock it with great solemnity. I'd hold my pen over the page.

"We had cheeseburgers for dinner." No, that was stupid.

"Sneezy [the guinea pig that introduced me to death as a wider concept] died." *I cried so much. My heart hurts. How on earth do I put that on paper so the words hold what I feel?*

"I want to be a dancer." This was actually untrue. I wanted to be a writer and a flight attendant, but all the popular girls at school wanted to be ballerinas, so I wrote it down.

Of course, I abandoned the locking diary the first time my sister broke into it. I don't blame her. I would have broken into hers, if she had one, in a hot minute. (Reminder: password protect your writing or computer!)

The magic was already gone from the diary, though, even before she broke in. I had learned that the book wouldn't make me a writer. I had thought that with a safe place to keep them, I'd have big thoughts. My sentences would be beautiful. Transformative.

Instead, they were just words about the very average me that I was, and as such, they were deeply disappointing. I wasn't Louisa May Alcott because I got a diary. Instead, I was seven-year-old Rachael with stick-straight brown hair who threw up in public places. Often.

Since then, I've tried it all. Morning pages (years of them, all in a box, all incredibly painful and boring. I can't bear to read more than a few sentences every few years. The twenties are hard for everyone, right? Yow). Moleskine journals. Digital pens. Diary apps on my phone. Online journals (okay, that one kind of stuck. I still blog and lately have started sharing bits of my current morning pages there).

Through it all? No matter what method I've tried, I still end up a disappointment to myself. I lie in bed and think Great Huge Thoughts about Life and The Universe. I get to the page and end up transferring only peanut butter smears and misspelled words.

The things I write in my journal aren't profound. Maybe you recognize the feeling?

Last year I read *The Folded Clock*, by Heidi Julavits. Now, Julavits *is* profound. I loved how she shaped her journal into literature. The things she saw meant something. She shifted so smoothly, so gracefully, from living life to observing it and back into life. In a piece that's relevant to what *you're* doing right now:

"It was hard to tell the truth, is what I'm saying. I tried to tell it, but I was aware of how each sentence had a million conditional offshoots. Like if you were to diagram a sentence for meaning, rather than grammar, that's what each sentence might have resembled. I was trying to be charismatic, and in doing so I probably didn't tell the truthiest truths. I never made stuff up. But I did strive to be entertaining. Such embellishments do not constitute lies. They constitute your personality. But your personality can seem like a storefront for lie vending if what you've said threatens to find a wider audience." [23]

I tried to emulate Julavits—the visceral way she remembered details and then attached meaning to them. I really did. But I couldn't do it.

I *do* want a method to remember what happens to me, and I'm bad at that. So I'm currently utilizing Julia Cameron's morning pages again, from her book, *The Artist's Way*. (You write three pages, longhand, first thing in the morning. I'll admit to you I'm bending her main principle, and I do them on the computer because get-thee-behind-me-RSI-devil. I *did* use a free font-maker online to make a font of my own handwriting, and I write the morning pages in that. It feels different enough to me that I'm able to get out of my own way.) I'm printing it out, too, in a desperate bid to be able to read it in my far-off future without trying to figure out how to use an obsolete thumb drive (remember floppy disks? Got some writing on those?).

Someday, I'll flip through the pages and remember how Julie made mole to put on the turkey. I'll remember the way Lala's face looked when she told me about getting her raise. I'll remember the seven stitches my sister got when she cut her hand on broken glass the day before her cat died.

I don't have to write the pages well. They are ugly and lazy and full of typos and, most of all, it's full of things that wouldn't be worth anyone else's time to read.

But there are things worth remembering for *me*. There are so many of them. Even if you've gotten to this point unable to access most of your memories, you can start collecting them now, for the future.

In *The Writing Life*, Annie Dillard said, "How we spend our days is, of course, how we spend our lives."

That quote used to quite literally terrify me. I had it taped to my refrigerator for many years when I wasn't writing. I was so scared I would miss my chance, that I'd be someone who eventually gave up and said, "I used to dream of being a writer."

How do *you* keep track of your days?

Catch the stories as they happen. Because you write down events and details very close to the moment they happened, you can codify the story early, pinning it to the page like a butterfly. Remember when we talked about the fact that writing a memory solidifies it? You can do that when it's still fresh.

Use something like a Line-a-Day, one of those old one-line-per-day calendars. Do Julia Cameron's morning pages. Use an online app (but back it up securely!).

But catch the minutes somehow.

Catch both the explosions and the quiet exhalations.

You'll find a treasure that you can't predict. You'll harvest old, forgotten memories as you store the new ones. You'll be astonished how they flood in. I promise.

Chapter Eighteen

PRO TIPS

I bring you a gift! Here's a loose collection of the *most* important things to know when writing memoir! Or, really, when writing anything.

Be Visceral:

This might be the most crucial thing in this book. It's hidden back here for *you*, the person who makes it this far.

Being visceral on the page is what takes my students' writing from mediocre or good to outstanding.

So pay attention. Bringing the visceral into your writing is one of the easiest things to learn how to do, and it's one of the most important things for a writer to master, a happy combination.

Here's the truth about writing about people, yourself included. All of us respond viscerally to outer and inner stimuli. We can't help it. Like we've discussed, our lizard brains take over. If we're scared or happy or sad, our bodies react. And all humans react in very similar ways, no matter their culture.

- Anger: Our hearts race, heat flashes through our core, we sweat, our muscles shake.
- Happiness: We get breathless, we feel heat in our chests, we might feel lightweight or even weightless.
- Guilt: We get upset stomachs, tight chests, and we lose our appetites.

When you describe these and similar visceral feelings on the page, your reader understands what you're explaining much better than if you just told them the emotion you're trying to describe.

If you show the physical, internal reaction to that emotion to your reader, they get it on a DNA level.

Compare this:

I couldn't believe what my uncle had said. I felt ashamed.

To:

I stared at my uncle. My hands started to tremble, and my throat got thick with salt. My knees wobbled. I swallowed bile.

You, as the reader, *feel* more when reading the second one. Those strong words light up parts of your brain, and you can imagine what the character felt. I didn't tell you what her uncle had said, but I showed the character's visceral response, and that tells you everything you need to know about how she feels about it. *I felt ashamed* means little. Swallowing bile and trembling means a lot.

It's important to remember that *all* people in real life and *all* characters on the page have visceral responses to emotion.

Even people who are cut off from feeling their emotions in their heads (you know the ones; you might *be* one) still have visceral responses. They are autonomic and automatic. They cannot be prevented.

They're clues that you give the reader, and they're universal.

Visceral Hack:

Buy *The Emotion Thesaurus.*

The book lists seventy-five emotions (shame, anguish, irritation, anger, happiness, fear, wariness) and describes what happens in the body. THIS IS THE COOLEST THING EVER.

Not only does the book describe what's happening internally, but each section also describes what happens externally, so you can both describe how you feel *and* you can describe what you see other people do. So instead of saying Uncle John was furious, you might show his flaring nostrils or his fists clenching and unclenching.

I recommend buying the book on Kindle so that you can have it open on your computer when you write. You're not cheating— you won't copy word for word what it says. You'll use it to jog your memory of what you or others might have felt. It's an invaluable resource.

Master writing the visceral details of emotion, and you'll have your reader eating from your hand.

Be Specific in the Senses:

Similarly, you want to bring your reader in with sensory details (smell, sight, sound, touch, taste). The difference between visceral and sense details is that visceral is inward, universal, and unpreventable. Sense details are the way humans respond to exterior stimuli, and they are individual, particular to the character.

The details should be concrete and specific. Remember when we were talking about the lizard brain, we learned that reading sense words makes the reader's brain light up in the appropriate areas? *Use that.*

Compare this:

My brother's room was always stinky.

To:

My brother's room smelled like a combination of uncleaned hamster cage and nacho cheese. The overarching fog of Axe body spray hung over the mess like a sickly-sweet poison cloud, but that gas was no match for my brother's own, and the toxic combo made me gasp for fresh air.

Which is better? Which tells you more?

But Rachael, I can't remember exactly what it smelled like. I just know it stunk.

This is where you get to use that 80 percent rule. If it was forty years ago and you've forgotten those small details, use your imagination to figure out what the room *probably* smelled like. Did he drink a lot of milk? Would the room have smelled like forgotten glasses filled with an inch of sour milk? Make an educated guess that you think is likely to be true with an accuracy of 80 percent or more (trust your gut!) and call that good. Write it. This is your book, your memories, your beliefs.

But Rachael, if I'm too specific about all the details, will I lose the reader because they don't identify with my certain situation?

GREAT QUESTION! No.

You can't be too specific, ever.

James Joyce said, "In the particular is contained the universal."

The *more* specific you are about everything—about the dragon-head candle on the nightstand, about the way the house smelled like patchouli even when fish was frying—the more universally accessible your story becomes to your reader.

As Mary Karr says, "The reader gets zipped into your skin." [24]

An added bonus of specificity is an added level of believability. "The kitchen always smelled like tomatoes," is pretty good. But if I say, "The kitchen always smelled like garden tomatoes, a mix of dirt and redness and the thick, sour scent that came in off the vines. It reminded me of the smell of geraniums. It wasn't something I'd want a perfume made out of, but it was something I couldn't help liking along with the scent of gasoline and dry-erase markers. When Mom did her tomato canning for the year, I could smell the tomato vine all the way up into my brain, and I despaired of ever getting the scent out."

You were with me in that last sentence, comparing those smells I'm describing to the times you've smelled them. Those words on the page light up your olfactory cortex. You empathize and identify with me. This brings you along with me, which, as a writer, is my entire goal.

The more specific you are, the more universal your book becomes. Use the details. Wring them for everything they're worth. Your reader will love you for it.

Dialogue

Add dialogue every single place you can, using the 80 percent rule and the knowledge that recreated dialogue is acceptable in memoir. You don't have a photographic memory. You can't remember exactly what was said. None of us can. But you can aim for getting the room tone right and putting words into people's mouths that you know they would say.

Compare:

We had a fight, and my father told me I wasn't worth the very shoes I owned. I was frightened of him.

To:

"You think you actually *deserve* those shoes I bought you? You might be able to get over on your mother, but I know the truth." Dad leaned closer, and I felt his spittle land on my cheek as sweat broke on my brow. "She says you're mine. I know you're not. You'll wear those shoes till your toes are sticking out of the holes you wear in them, and then you'll patch them yourself. You're not getting another cent out of me, ever."

In the second example, we see the father spitting in fury. This is an exterior clue to his interior emotion (see above on visceral details), and it's universally understandable. We also see our main character breaking into a sweat. She doesn't have to say she's scared because we all understand visceral clues intuitively. Not only are we getting the actual voice of the father, we are inhabiting our main character's body, and we're rooting for her, all in one short paragraph.

This is one of the things I point out most in my students' work—the scenes in which they briefly mention what was said without using dialogue. Every time you have a chance to open up a scene, to breathe it into life with dialogue, do it.

But don't use filler.

"Hey," my brother said.
   "Hi," I said back.
   "How are you?" he asked.
   "Fine, thanks," I said.

You need none of this. You don't need hellos or goodbyes unless they tell us something concrete about the characters. Skip every line that doesn't help inform us of what you want us to know.

Of course, the above exchange *could* mean something, but only if you intend it to.

Compare the above to:

I was peeling potatoes. My brother walked into the kitchen and then just stood there, his hands open, flexing.

"Hey," he said.

Nothing good ever came from him saying *hey*. He was looking for trouble.

"Hi." I hoped I was wrong.

He rapped his knuckles against the kitchen table. A simple threat. "How are you?"

He didn't care how I was. He never had. "Fine, thanks." What a lie. I'd never been worse. But it wasn't something I'd ever share with him.

In this example, it's fine to write prosaic, boring, everyday dialogue because there's something bigger behind it, something you as the author get to show the reader. Using dialogue to say what's *not* being said is an advanced trick, but guess what? You're good at it already. We all participate in this hiding/revealing of meaning in every conversation we have. Explore this subext in your book.

Exercise:

Dialogue

Call a relative. Have a chat. Do not record it, and don't try too hard to memorize what's discussed.

As soon as you hang up, write a few notes to yourself about

what was said, and more importantly, what was said without words.

Expand this into a scene. You don't have to use this in your memoir (in fact, you probably won't), but while you write the scene, pretend you will. Include only the info that helps you get your meaning across.

Point of View

Put simply, you've got to stay in your own lane. You can only describe what *you* know. If you say, "I was scared," we can believe you (but show us viscerally, huh?). If you say, "Mom was scared," then you *must* show us why you believe that. Either she can tell you that in dialogue, or you can extrapolate it from physical clues, but you can't headhop into her point of view (POV). If you enter Mom's POV, you're making something up out of whole cloth, and even if you're right about how she feels, it can be read as a lie. Don't lie to your reader. They'll know and close the book.

Example:

Mom was angry. She thought about all the times he'd come home late, and the way she'd felt the time he got picked up by the cops.

I can't trust this memoirist. She hasn't told me what evidence shows her that Mom was angry, and the memoirist simply can't know what her mother was thinking (unless she was told in dialogue).

The only POV you can work with in memoir is first person.

Okay, that's not *entirely* true. Here's what Beth Kephart says about this: "Experiment with form. Memoir isn't always a first-person tale. Mark Richard and others have proven the power of a second-person memoir. bell hooks shows what can happen when several different voices tell a single true story. Graphic memoirists capture the past with the images they draw. Give yourself permission to produce a non-traditional memoir. You may return to the first-person pronoun in the end. But you will have given yourself room to make an informed decision." [25]

Truly, you'll probably go with first-person unless you're Being Experimental, in which case, go with your bad self, Dada.

But bear with me for a minute. I'm going to lay a big thought on you here.

No matter what, in your memoir, you're two things— you're both the main character and the narrator. (I know. It's mind-bending.)

Phillip Lopate said, "In writing memoir, the trick, it seems to me, is to establish a double perspective that will allow the reader to participate vicariously in the experience as it was lived (the child's confusions and misapprehensions, say), while benefiting from the sophisticated wisdom of the author's adult self. This second perspective, which takes advantage of a more mature intelligence to interpret the past, is not merely an obligation but a privilege and an opportunity. In any autobiographical narrative, whether memoir or personal essay, the marrow often shows itself in those moments where the writer analyzes the meaning of his or her experience." [26]

Yes, feel free to write in the voice of a five-year-old, but know that it's okay to use the adult wisdom you gained by being that child. Or you may choose to leave out the narrator's wisdom until later in the book. You make the rules. Just remember, there's the you of the past, and the you sitting in that writing chair. You're the one in charge of mixing that character and that narrator into the robustness of your memoir.

Tense

This is an easy one—it's author's choice! You can write in present tense, though that can imply a chronological progression you might not stick to. More common is the use of past tense. This gives a greater ease in jumping around in time. I'm quite fond of splitting books into two timelines: a "now" in present tense, and a chronological past-tense "then."

And I'll be controversial here: tense is an easy thing to change in revision (though it's tedious, changing all those "ares" to "weres" or vice versa). So play around. What feels best as you write? Does it slip into and out of past and present? That's okay. Your editor will help with this later. Just get it written.

Chapter Nineteen

WORRY BUSTING

So.

Let's talk.

props head on hands

Are you getting through it? Do you have some words on the page? Are you getting a little frantic and wide-eyed at the thought that you're not doing this right?

Quick! Let's bust some worries!

I'm not a good enough writer to do this. I'm a fraud.

Okay, bear with me. Maybe that's true! You might not be getting things right in this, the first draft. But let's go back to the Susan Sontag quote: "What I write is smarter than I am, because I can rewrite it." You should have piles of crap on the page, and you will fix all of that later. Now you're just going for capturing lots and lots of *terrible* words. You can do that, right?

I don't have enough story. Everyone else was lost on a mountain/hideously abused/a war hero, but all I have is a story about being a mom. No drama.

Don't worry about this. Personally, I'd rather read a quiet memoir over a war memoir any day. There's enough drama in just getting through a routine Monday to satisfy me as a reader. Show me the moments in your life. Make them real. Make them completely specific to you (thus making them universally understandable), and I'll care terribly.

I'm worried I won't follow through and finish.

Valid worry. Bookmark this spot.

Time for a little tough love.

There are, literally, millions of people who would like to write their memoir. Some of them start. The vast majority of them fail to finish or even to get more than a chapter or two written. You could easily fall into this group and vanish without a trace.

- The only thing that will help is for you to do the work.
- The only way to get the work done is to keep showing up and putting terrible words on the page that you'll fix later.
- The only way to keep showing up is to put a daily or weekly word count or page goal on your calendar *and then do the work.* It's hard. It doesn't feel good.

I can't actually talk you into doing it (though I am trying to). No one can. *You* have to find the time, and it's okay if you don't. No one will miss your memoir not existing.

But people might be changed by your memoir if you *do* write it.

So, as John Scalzi says, "Do you want to write, or don't you? If your answer is 'yes, but,' then here's a small editing tip: what you're doing is using six letters and two words to say 'no.' And that's fine. Just don't kid yourself as to what 'yes, but' means." [27]

Go ahead and read that quote again.

It's fine if you don't write your book. But I think you should. You're the one responsible for getting it done, no one else. And I know you *can* do it.

I'm scared of failing.

Of course you are! I put off writing for years because it was the only thing I really wanted to do. If I gave it my full effort and I failed, then I felt my life might not be worth living. (I never thought it out in these words. If you'd asked me then why I wasn't serious about writing, I would have given you a dozen excuses, all of them mostly false.)

Here's the thing about books: you will indubitably fail at writing the book you want to write. The image we have in our mind about what we want our books to be never comes to perfect fruition, ever. And that's okay, because when you finish your book, you'll have the *right* book in your hands. It will change into the book it was meant to be. That's not failing. That's the pinnacle of success.

People will hate me if I write this stuff.

Maybe so. Maybe not. Don't worry about that now. Just write it
and later decide what to do with it. Read the Family section again.

**You keep saying I'll revise it later, but I don't know how to
revise.**

Oh, my friend, I've got you. The next chapter walks you right
through it, and revision is *the best*.

**I've started, but I've lost my mojo. I don't think I'll get
it back.**

Brute force, my friends. Brute force. (Mojo is over there with the
muse, laughing at the way you believe in them. Flip them the bird.
It feels good.)

Show up. Sit down and write. Bash the words out. Claw them
out of your soul with a pickaxe. Promise yourself the best scotch
you can afford if you can just finish five more scenes. Get a writer
friend to meet you, and while you're pounding your quad-shot
Venti latte, tell him he can't let you go to the bathroom until
you've written a thousand words.

There is no mojo. There's just sitting down and getting some
terrible words on the page.

You can do this.

I know you can.

Chapter Twenty

REVISION

"Now, we talk about revision," I say, writing REVISION on the whiteboard in red dry-erase letters.

I hear a low *whoosh*.

I turn back to the class to see that all seats have been evacuated. I hear screaming in the halls as my students race for their cars. A single abandoned pencil rolls off a desk, clattering to the floor. Dust rises. I weep.

Knock it off.

Revision is the *best*.

Seriously. The reason you don't know this yet is just that you haven't done very much of it. You might never have revised a book before. I don't think I'd ever truly revised anything before I started completing books. In my former life as a trying-but-failing writer, I thought revision was going through what I'd written and making sure the sentences were as pretty as I could make them and that they contained as few typos as possible.

True revision, in which a writer takes apart a book and puts it back together again, terrified me. I knew I couldn't do it. How could *anyone* pull it off?

I'll tell you how: step by step, little by little, just like you wrote the book.

And truthfully, you will *have* to revise. You'll have to do it the big way, the taking apart and putting back together way. You'll have to toss out scenes you love and write new ones that are better. There no way around this. But I think it's way more fun that first-drafting. We might agree to disagree, but let's have that argument after you've done it.

What I adore about revision is this: I know the world. I invented it, after all! When I open the document, I'm right in the middle of something I understand. It's much easier for me to drop in for hours and rest on the page. It's also easier to come out of, to shake off and rejoin the world.

First drafts remain torture for me. I can admit that *sometimes* the writing of new words is glorious. You surprise yourself with a turn of phrase that you're pretty sure is genius and has probably never been said before. The plot bends and a tree you wrote about comes to life and points a branched finger in a direction you never saw coming. Inspiration flows, hot and heavy.

But maybe I'm just more of a down-to-earth gal. I love falling in love, but I love remaining in love more. Give me a passionate kiss before you take the trash out—that's happiness to me. I like the comfort of what I know. I like to tuck my feet under the thighs of my manuscript as we cuddle on the couch. I love knowing my manuscript likes the lights on till sleep-time, even though I prefer to read in the dark.

Revision is both comfortable and exciting, like a sturdy marriage. Oh, I love the word *sturdy*. It's prosaic, but so am I. My legs are sturdy. My emotions are, too. I love my books to be sturdy enough to lean on.

And lean on them, I do. I fall into them. Revisions are getting in the bed you made of out words and pulling up the covers. Then you roll around, making those words better, stronger, more focused.

Revision is when the *really* big ideas show up. Then you move parts around—like those flat puzzle toys where you slide pieces around to make a picture—to make the new ideas fit. You might have to pry out some pieces and manufacture new ones. But then you click one piece left and another one right, and suddenly, you're looking at it.

You see the whole picture. Your book.

Macro Revision

This is the important stuff.

You do this BEFORE you make the sentences pretty. This comes first.

When you're in macro revision, you're looking at your book structurally.

- Does it have the body you meant it to have?
- Have you clothed it the way you wanted to?
- Does it stand on its own legs?
- Can it do the things you want it to?

Imagine you're able to get above your book and look down at it from a bird's-eye view. You can't see the typos—instead, you can see the ways in which you can make the whole stronger.

You're used to being on the ground, in the weeds, struggling to write good scenes. Being able to look down and move those scenes around so they work together can seem impossible.

But again, step by step, you'll get there. Here's how.

1. Find Your Theme

We talked a lot about writing either a time-based or a theme-based memoir. This is *not* the same kind of theme (ah, those tricky writing words that serve multiple purposes). When I say "theme" here, I mean the overall message of your book. Now that your first draft is done, I want you to find a simple theme that defines what you're trying to pull off with this memoir. I want you to be able to encapsulate your entire book in just a few words.

Examples:
Love heals all wounds.
Love heals no wounds.
Family is strongest when chosen.
Pain leads to growth.

What's your theme for this memoir? Write it down now. If you'd like your reader to take away one universal statement about the way you look at the world, what would that be?

This is essential. You can't skip this part.

Got it? Good. Now write it on a small Post-it and smack it onto the top of your computer. As you revise, you'll be holding up every single scene to see if your theme is illustrated. More on this in a moment.

2. Print it out

Yes, all of it. Print it so that the lines are separated by at least 1.5 lines—double-spaced is even better. I like to triple-hole punch that big stack and put them in a binder. I like to flip through them with my eyes slightly closed and think to myself, *I wrote ALL of these dang words!* Then I like to find my favorite pen and sit on my big cushy blue chair in the living room with a mug of tea.

When you do this, please have at hand a *ton* of small Post-its. I like the standard 2 x 1.5-inch kind that you can easily steal from work. Have more than you think you'll need. Prepare yourself to color code or not (I don't—I'll happily use any color as long as they're sticky).

3. Read the Whole Thing

You might feel sick of the story, but it *will* look different printed out, I promise. Read it from beginning to end, no skipping.

Important:

Ignore typos. Don't change sentences at this point. Just read.

If you can't bear to overlook the typos, only let yourself make a check mark next to the line that needs to be fixed later. The reason you don't let yourself fix anything at the granular level right now is this: thinking about how to spell "guess" correctly will crash you down from the bird's-eye view and bring you right back into the writing trench. That's not what we want. We want to stay soaring above for a while longer.

But Rachael, I'll forget to make the change if I don't fix it at that moment.

No, you won't.

First, your eye is remarkably reliable. You'll always see the same errors and think of the same fixes because your voice is your voice is your voice, as I've mentioned. Trust that.

Second, if you make the words too perfect now, you'll be loath to throw them out later if you need to.

Third, copy editors are better than you'll ever be at checking your work. They're imperative. Rely on them (but later).

4. Sentence Outline

This is the secret weapon of revision!

This puts the eye in that bird we've been talking about—this is how you get off the ground and into the air to get a real, true look at your memoir.

While you read through your book, make a list of your scenes. Don't look at your earlier outline, and don't guess. List each scene as you come to it, summing it up in just a few words. It can be messy. The phrases don't have to make sense to anyone else, just you.

Yours might look something like this:

1. Mom, dad, bacon on porch

2. The fire

3. When John and I met

4. John meeting Mom, the ice

You keep going, keep reading, jotting a phrase or two for each and every scene you encounter. There's no judgment at this time. Just write it down.

So you're reading. You're writing down phrases.

What do you do if you have a big idea?

5. The Beauty of Post-its

Another piece of magic, friends: write the big idea down on a small Post-it. Again, I'm talking the 2 x 1.5-inch Post-it, the small, rectangular ones.

But this idea is so awesome it won't fit on a bitty note like that.

Yes, it will. If you have more than a small Post-it to write it on, you'll lose momentum. Distill this great idea into four or five words, write them on a single Post-it, attach that Post-it to a piece of binder paper, or into your writing journal, and move on.

Don't get attached to these ideas. You're going to be having a lot of them, and many of them won't work out in the long run. That's okay, just keep reading, writing your sentence outline, and jotting down Post-it notes. They're safe there.

6. Actually Starting Revision

You're now 99 percent more equipped than most writers are when they stare into the open maw of revision. Take a moment to feel proud of that fact. Feel your chest swell.

Now the real fun begins.

Print out that list of scenes, your sentence outline (if you've been keeping this by hand, that's fine, but quick-like-a-bunny type it up now, double-spaced).

Read it.

There.

You just took about two minutes to read your entire book.

And I bet you're feeling some things. You realize that the back end of the book is too heavy with stories about your husband, whereas you want this to be more about you and your mom. Or you see that you need more about basic training and Iraq and less about Afghanistan.

Even better, while reading, you make an association you've never seen before. Oh, shit, the problem you had at that job was directly related to the problem you had as an eight-year-old on the playground! How could you not have seen that before now?

Start to draw all over it. Mark it up. Draw arrows. Write bubbles of dialogue you hear in your head. Make connections.

Look at the story structure chapter again and think about those four boxes. See if you can slide scenes around to help you create a stronger story arc. Keep in mind those turning points— see if you can find them in your outline.

- Can you find the 20-25 percent mark, when something took you out of your normal routine, pushing you into Reaction?
- Can you find the 50 percent context-shifting midpoint when you moved into Action?
- Can you find the 75-80 percent Dark Moment when all was lost?

Mark these on your sentence outline.

Pro tip: It's possible you're doing multiple timelines, a common practice in memoir, shifting from then to now to a different then. **Consider each timeline a thread and weave them together in your book.** Can you slide scenes around so that all the timelines hit their marks at approximately the best location? If you're writing about your relationship with your now-dead dad and also the relationship with your current wife, can you make sure the Dark Moment of each will occur at around 75-80 percent of the way through, word-count-wise? This is advanced, but you might be surprised how things start lining up for you as you shift and juggle scenes. (Scrivener is *wildly* useful for this kind of juggling.)

While looking at your sentence outline, ask yourself what-ifs.

- *What if I moved the Dad section to the beginning? It wouldn't be chronological then, but does that feel better to me?*
- *What if I didn't talk about Egypt at all? I think it might not fit.*
- *What if I moved the boat trip to the end?*
- *What if this book isn't about me and my aunt at all, but about the way I respond to female influence?*

Yeah, you might have some big surprises when you start scribbling over the outline. Be open to them. You might even change the theme you drafted in the first part of this chapter. That's okay.

After you've given your all to that outline, after it's covered in scribbles and ideas, go back and update that outline file.

Make your outline what you *want* your book to be. On mine, I make it clear what I need to change in revision by putting all the changes that need to happen in bold, so I don't miss them. Other people use different colors or fonts. You do you.

This is a great time to bring in outside help. Don't ask other writers to read your whole memoir yet—you want to get it into better shape before you do (unless you've already been work-shopping with a class or group). But do ask a writer friend or three to look over your new outline (these need to be writers, not just friends or family). Meet for coffee and explain it to them, since they won't understand what your outline abbreviations are.

Ask them to be honest.

- What are they missing?
- What do they want to read more about?
- What connections don't they understand?
- Do they see the story arc?
- Do they have ideas for a better way to map it out?

When you're done with your new outline, you have a map for your revisions.

Isn't that *awesome*? Isn't this *exactly* what you needed? Again, you're 99 percent ahead of writers who open their books to revise then run out of the room screaming in fear.

You're going to rewrite your book to fit your ideal outline.

You'll rewrite your book to fit your theme.

How? Start at the beginning.

Open your document or Scrivener file and do a SAVE AS. Make yourself feel better. Save this new revision as a new project. That way, your finished first draft is always safe. Start clean. Save as. Did I mention save as? Do a save as.

Move scenes around now to match your new outline. Again, this is easy in Scrivener.

Look at the very first scene. Ask yourself (and check your gut for the answer; it knows):

- Is this necessary?
- Does this fit with my theme? (This is why your theme is stuck to your computer on that little Post-it. If the scene doesn't illustrate or expand upon your theme, you'll need to fix it so that it does. This will make your book cohere. For example, in this book I'm not talking about how to garden. Gardening isn't my theme. Writing memoir is.)
- Am I *positive* that this is the way I want to open?

If the answer is no, send that scene to:

The Cuts File

This is what I call it on my computer. Other people call it the Dump, the Bonus Scenes, the Garbage, the Save For Later file. I have a friend who calls it the I'll Use Every Gorgeous Word in Here file. Call it what you like. In Scrivener, you can just delete the scene, and it automatically lands—very safely—in the Trash File.

Those words are secure. They're not going anywhere.

Tell yourself you'll go back and fish all those words out and put them in the right place someday. (This is a lie. I can count on one hand the times I've gone into the trash to pull something out. But this lie is a sweet one, and it comforts me.)

If that first scene isn't exactly right, move the whole thing to the Cuts file. You're allowed to copy and paste out what *does* feel right about the scene into a new first scene. Bring along the words that work. Maybe the first three paragraphs are killer, but the end of the scene is weak. Great. Bring into the new revision only those first three paragraphs, dump them into the new scene, and write around them. Forget the words in the trash and write new ones.

Because you're starting from something that's all you, something you've already partially breathed to life, this will feel exciting. It might also feel overwhelming. But I guarantee this will be more fun than you thought it would be—because you did the prep work. You have that gorgeous new outline, your roadmap to success.

When you're satisfied with the first scene, do the same with the next one, referring to your outline and theme as anchors. Throw out what you don't love. Add words that you do.

You're going to adore this part of the writing. To me, this is when I truly feel like a real writer. To me, this is when it's *fun*.

Other good things to ask of each scene:

- Can I combine this scene with any other scene? Oh, the joy of combining scenes for maximum awesomeness. It feels *great* to do this.
- Can I enter the scene a little later? Can I get out earlier? Trust your reader. Don't show them the way you walk up the porch and ring the doorbell unless this helps illustrate something important. If the fight with

your best friend happens inside, get us inside that apartment faster. Get us out quick. Keep the pace tight and keep it moving.

- Am I keeping this scene just because I love it? Am I keeping it because I'm proud of my writing, or because it's super funny? Is it necessary? Does it move my story forward? Hey, even if it's the best writing you've ever done, if it doesn't fit in your outline and help illustrate your theme, toss it into the Save For Later file. You can revise it to be a personal essay, perhaps. Maybe you can send it to Modern Love. But if your gut says it doesn't belong, then it doesn't. Don't try to fool your gut. That thing is smart and knows more than you do.

Getting to the End of the Macro Revision

I know it's not as simple as I'm making this sound, but honestly, you just keep doing the same thing, over and over, till you get to the end.

Lift out a scene. Hold it up to the light and look at it. Is it perfect? Great. If it's not, move it to the Cuts File, and build a new one from the ashes of the first.

It will feel like it takes *forever*, I know that.

But take comfort in this truth: the first half of your revision will be the slowest part. While you're making these big choices about how to restructure your memoir and deciding what goes in and what stays out, you're narrowing your exit. The further you go into the revision, the faster you'll go. By the end of the revision, it will feel like skiing downhill on a crisp, sunny morning when the powder is fresh and you're the only one on the mountain. Your speed will astound you.

But yeah, if it feels like you're crawling through mud on your belly for a while at the beginning, that's normal.

Trust your gut.

Do the work.

You *can* do this. You already did the hard parts! Revision is nerve-racking, but it's *way* easier than writing the whole first draft. You've got this.

The Draft Passes:

Now you get to do something I take great joy in: doing draft passes.

Some of us are good at certain things, and others are good at other things. None of us are good at everything. Personally, I'm terrible at including setting in my scenes. I have terrible cases of "heads in space," in which my characters just talk to each other as if they're suspended in a completely blank room. I used to worry about this and struggle through each scene trying to add setting. Now I don't. I just do a Settings Pass in which I go quickly through each scene and make sure the setting is vivid. I do this at the end. It takes maybe an hour to insert this into a whole book, fiction or memoir.

Isn't that tricky? Doesn't that feel like you're cheating a little bit? Nope, it's just a tool! Harness this to help your own weaknesses.

Other people use draft passes to check and fix things like:

- Dialogue—Can more be added?
- Visceral details—Can the reader feel the main character's emotions simply through bodily, visceral details?

- Point of View—Do you ever slip into knowing something about other people that you couldn't have known for sure?
- Tense—Do you keep the tense consistent?
- Passive voice—Is your manuscript mostly clear of the passive voice?
- Setting—As mentioned, are we solidly in the world? Can we see, hear, taste, smell, touch the environment? Be specific to be universal.
- Truthfulness—Especially in memoir, a draft pass is a great time to evaluate each sentence for veracity. Even if you're piecing together memories and recreating dialogue, ask yourself if each scene is *honest*, to the best of your ability.
- Humor—Some writers don't write humor easily. If you feel your book is too dark, go back and inject levity where you naturally can. It's odd to do it this way, but you might be a person who writes sparely in the first draft and expands in the second draft.
- Seriousness—Same as above, but flipped. Too much light? Add some dark. It's about balance.

For example, if you're injecting humor because you feel you should, you might come across something like this:

It was snowing, the air frozen and bitter, the day we lost Pat.

After your humor pass, it might read like this:

Snow fell from the sky like cold, white confetti that morning. The air made my snot congeal, and when I wiped my nose with the back of my mitten, I could almost hear my frozen nostril-hairs crunch. Pat wasn't even our dog, he was borrowed. The three of us kids were pet-sitting him, which meant that we all forgot to fill his food bowl. When we realized it, we fought for the right to feed him, elbowing each other out of the way. Pat was bemused, patient, and then, very suddenly, gone.

You can do this with each pass. It's labor-intensive, and honestly, it's also lots of fun.

Micro Revision

I know, you thought you were done. I'm sorry, not quite.

After you get your scenes in the right order, after you include the things you want to include and toss out what you don't, *now* you finally get to make those sentences sing.

This is why I haven't been nagging you to make gorgeous sentences until now: if you make each sentence or paragraph perfect, you'll find a "need" to use it. That won't serve you well. It's hard to throw out lines you've slaved over, lines that are truly beautiful.

But now that you're at the final stage, you finally get to go through each sentence and make it a little better. I like to imagine I'm putting each sentence into a Twitter box (sad but true). Can I take out words? Can I use better ones? Can I make this sentence funnier, or more poignant, or happier?

You also finally get to worry about typos (but not too hard—you'll need to hire a copy editor, or if you sell the book traditionally, the publisher will hire one for you, and they'll help you with this. No one can see their own errors. Trust me on this).

The Second Draft is Complete.

It is? *You are amazing.*

Celebrate. This is always my favorite celebration, even better than writing "The End." Having a clean draft to send to my editor or agent is the best feeling in the world. It's the "truck draft," which is what Jennifer Crusie calls the version of the book that's not completely perfect yet but could be published if she got hit by a truck.

And holy crap on a popsicle stick. What next?

Chapter Twenty-One

HOW TO PUBLISH

What Next?

Let's talk (very briefly) about publishing. This book is *not* about how to get published. There are a million resources and good books out there. I'll list some below, but I'll also give you the quickest overview of today's publishing industry ever.

We live in the best time that's ever existed for publishing. I mean that very seriously. Our human ancestors have been around for two million years, painting their memoirs on cave walls. Modern man has been around for 200,000 years. Written language has only existed for 3,000 of those. The internet has only been around for twenty-seven years, and e-publishing has only been a viable system for the last ten. The fact that, in two million years, you just *happen* to be living in the ten that allow for mass distribution of *your story?* Dude, that's incredible, right?

There are two ways to go when you want to publish your book:

1. Traditional publishing
2. Self-publishing.

Writers who do both are called hybrid authors. I'm a hybrid author. I traditionally publish my mainstream fiction worldwide. I traditionally publish some of my romances. Other romances I self-publish. Some of my creative non-fiction is traditionally published, and other works of non-fiction, like this book, I choose to hire out my editing (because editing is always, always necessary) and self- publish.

Traditional Publishing

Over the last couple of decades, traditional publishers have been merging into larger and larger conglomerates. The Big Five are (at the time of this writing):

1. Penguin Random House (They really missed a great opportunity when they didn't choose to rename themselves Random Penguin, in my opinion)
2. Simon & Schuster
3. HarperCollins
4. MacMillan
5. Hachette

Within each of these five publishing houses are hundreds of imprints, which are just trade names that form a kind of umbrella company within the company. For example, when I was with HarperCollins, my books came out under the William Morrow imprint. Other William Morrow books were similar to mine (mainstream literary women's fiction). Each of those hundreds of imprints publishes hundreds of books a year, for a total of approximately 300,000 new traditional titles a year. (I know. It's mind-boggling.)

Here's where it gets a little tricky: the term "traditional publishing" *also* includes small, independent presses, like Haymarket, Graywolf, and Tin House Press. These are called indie presses. Some of them are just as prestigious as the Big Five and will have the same (or even better) distribution into bookstores.

In order to get a publishing contract with the Big Five, you *must* have an agent (more on that below). There are no exceptions, unless you have a million social media followers, in which case, they'll come to you. However, you don't necessarily need an agent to sell your book to the smaller indie presses.

Traditional publishing has a cachet that self-publishing still doesn't have. It's okay if this is what you want (it's what I wanted). It's harder to break in, but it can still be done, even if you know no one in the industry. I was a slush-pile baby, which means my manuscript was pulled out of a large stack on an agent's desk and "found" by an intern, who passed it on to my agent, who read it, who signed with me. My agent then went on to help me revise it (again) and then sold my book to an editor at HarperCollins, who then helped me revise it (yet again). My first book hit bookstore shelves eighteen months after my agent sold it to my editor, four years after I started writing it. This is a common time-frame. Traditional publishing is *slow*.

The biggest benefit of traditional publishing is distribution.

The Big Five will place you in national book chains (okay, Barnes & Noble is almost all we've got left) and in many independent bookstores. They do some publicity, but if you look at the above number of books they produce annually, you can see how the onus of publicity still falls to the author. You're the only author in your house, but you're one of the hundreds of authors in *their* house. So if you want to be traditionally pubbed so that you don't have to worry about marketing, you'll have to reset that expectation.

It's still really freaking cool to walk into a bookstore and find your book on the shelf. I have to admit, every time it happens to me, I want to tell the person standing in the aisle next to me, "Psst. I wrote this."

(Okay, I'll admit I did that once. The woman was completely startled and perhaps a little scared, but she was polite and said nice things like, "You're kidding! That's wonderful!" She left the aisle very quickly. I'm still embarrassed.)

In traditional publishing, you normally receive an advance, which is technically an advance on earnings. Basically, they're gambling on you. You make approximately 8-12 percent of the book's cover price (this is an oversimplification for the sake of conciseness).

If you get a $5,000 advance (an average advance for a new author, if not a little high—publishing isn't a get-rich-quick scheme), the publisher is saying they expect to sell enough of your books that you'll earn at least $5,000 in royalties—that is, your 8-12 percent of the cover price.

If you don't sell that much, you don't have to pay back the advance (you only have to do that if you fail to deliver a viable product to them by their specific due date).

If you sell *more* than your advance, you're said to have "earned out," and for every book that sells after you earn out, you'll receive a royalty paid to you, usually biannually. Of this amount, your agent, if you have one, takes a standard 15 percent (or 20 percent of foreign royalties).

Pro tip: Never, *ever* pay someone to publish your book. If you do, you're at risk of vanity publishing. There are many predators out there, waiting to get rich off your naivety. Run whatever publisher you're not sure about through the websites Writer Beware or Absolute Write to see if it's legit. If you go the traditional route, you get paid when your book sells, as does your agent. The only thing most agents ask you to pay is office/mailing fees, *nothing* else.

How to Get an Agent for Traditional Publishing

Go to AgentQuery.com. There, you can sort agents by who's looking for what genre. Each agent will tell you exactly what they want you to send them (the first three pages, the first fifty, just a query letter, a query and a synopsis, etc.). Follow their instructions to the letter.

Send your query letter (Google "How to Write a Darn Good Query Letter" and look for the NY Editors one) to as many agents as you can stand to hear rejections from. Use a spreadsheet or use QueryTracker.net to keep track of who asks for a partial or full manuscript. No response is—sadly—considered a No these days. The vast majority of your rejections will be no responses. It took me thirty-two attempts to get my agent, whom I love. It took John Grisham forty. It took my friend Sophie a hundred. It's a numbers game, and you just keep trying. When I was looking for an agent, I sent out five queries at a time because that was my personal limit for rejection. I couldn't handle six rejections in a week.

Self-Publishing

While it still doesn't have the cachet that traditional publishing has (though that's changing every year), self-publishing is a great way to go. As of just this year, there's almost nothing you *can't* do in self-publishing.

- You can release your e-book worldwide on platforms that include Amazon, Barnes & Noble, iBooks, Kobo, and Google Play (as well as a myriad of other smaller distributors).
- You can distribute print books, on demand, worldwide, of a quality that is just as good as traditional print books.
- You can hire narrators and release audiobooks with relative ease (through ACX, Amazon's Audible self-publishing platform, or other services).
- You can get distribution through Ingram Spark into independent bookstores and libraries.

And best of all, on e-books (the vast majority of self-publishing sales), you get a royalty of 35-70 percent. That's a whole heck of a lot better than 8-12.

Personally, I make way more money on my self-published romance than I do any of my traditional titles. I kind of think of romance as my day job, the thing I do that allows me to take risks on traditionally published titles in other genres.

Things to Know

You don't need an agent to self-publish. You keep all royalties.

That said, you might choose to pursue an agent for things like film rights and foreign deals.

Self-publishing is a lot of hard work with a steep learning curve.

What do you have to do when you're a self-published author (also called indie authors, not to be confused with indie presses mentioned above)?

- You have to complete and revise your manuscript to the best of your ability.
- You must hire out edits. For the love of God, do not *ever* publish anything you haven't had professionally edited. Edits include:
- Developmental edit: This is essential for a new writer. You can't skip this, and it's not cheap. Expect to pay $800-2000 for this.
- Copy edit: This is also one hundred percent essential. You can't skip this, but it's cheaper.
- Check out Reedsy.com. Most of their editors come from a traditional publishing background, and all are vetted.
- You must hire a graphic designer to make your cover.
- Let me be really clear about this: do *not* do this yourself. Even if you're an excellent graphic designer by trade, unless you're actually working in publishing, within the genre you're writing in, you *must* hire out a cover. The cover is how you sell a book. No matter what you think looks good, if it doesn't tell a browsing customer in a single, quarter-second glance what your book is about, your book will fail.

- Covers range from $150-1000.
- **Always, always, always hire out editing and cover design. Period.**
- You must choose your level of distribution.
- You must buy your own ISBNs (depending on where you live, this might be free. In the U.S., they're sold by Bowker, and they're expensive). You can publish without one on some platforms, but I wouldn't advise this.
- You must either learn to professionally format your interiors or hire this out. (This has been made easy to do yourself now by a product called Vellum, which I can't recommend more highly. You can do this quickly and beautifully now without needing to code anything yourself.)
- You must compile the metadata (literally, the data about your data) for your book, including category, BISAC listings, and keywords.
- You must upload to each platform (or use an aggregator like Draft2Digital or Publish Drive).
- You must do your own promotion and marketing, including things like email list building, paid advertisement, and giveaways.
- And if you're interested in writing another book, you're doing that *while* you're doing all of the above.

I know I've just scared the pants off you, but I did it for a reason.

There's a persistent rumor floating around out there that you can self-publish and rake in the dough. There *was* a time this was true, but unfortunately, the gold rush is over.

However, take heart!

Good writing finds readers. Your book can still sell, and it can sell well. It's all about how *you* choose to market and promote it, but it's excitingly viable. I honestly love self-publishing—I love all the tiny things that have to happen to make something work. I've loved teaching myself the process, and I get enjoyment from every part of it.

If you choose to self-publish, yes, you'll have to figure out all of the above, but it's all learnable when broken into small pieces, I promise. It can be done.

Recommended Titles:

Successful Self-Publishing, Joanna Penn
    Business for Authors, Joanna Penn
    Write, Publish, Repeat, Sean Platt, Johnny B. Truant, David Wright
    Let's Get Digital, David Gaughran

Interestingly enough, these are all self-published books, and they're great. Also, if you're into the idea of self-publishing, start mainlining podcasts like *The Creative Penn*, *The Sell More Books Show*, and *The Career Author*. Your brain will explode with the information, and you'll be overwhelmingly confused, and then it will settle down. You'll start to assimilate all the info. I find podcasts invaluable sources of industry information. (I also host two you might like, *How Do You Write*, about writing processes, and *The Petal to the Metal*, about living the life of a writer, cohosted with J. Thorn.)

There's So Much More!

But this isn't the book for teaching you about publishing.

AND BESIDES! You shouldn't worry about one single thing in this chapter until your book is written and revised. You can't sell an unwritten memoir on proposal unless you have an enormous social media/publicity platform, so unless you do, don't try.

You just have to write.

And I *know* you can do that.

Chapter Twenty-Two

THE LAST WORD

Dearest memoirist (because you get to call yourself that, you know),

Your story matters.

The world needs it.

There is no one but *you* who can write your story. There are people desperate to know that they can make it through what they're going through, the thing you conquered. Your book could save their lives.

Or perhaps your book will be a little quieter—maybe it will make someone forget that they're in a hospital bed. Maybe they'll laugh while reading what *you* wrote. What greater honor is there than that—to distract a worried and heavy mind? How worthy and how magnificent a gift that is to give someone?

And the one thing I know for sure is this: I can't put together sentences like you can. No one in the whole world can—not one person who's ever lived on this planet has *your* unique sensibilities and your ability to craft words into phrases, sentences, paragraphs, pages, and finally, into BOOKS.

I want you to do this.

I don't want you to read this book and become inspired and then fail to launch.

I want you to do the work.

Louis L'Amour said, "Start writing, no matter what. The water doesn't flow until you turn on the faucet."

It's hard work! I've made that damn clear, haven't I? Sorry about that. But you've learned I value truth, and you would think less of me if I lied to you about this.

But writing is the *best* work that exists. I think firefighting and midwifery are incredible jobs, but even an astronaut's job doesn't hold a single itty-bitty candle to the job we get to do when we sit at the page and tell our stories.

The ability and the desire to write came to you for a reason.

You're burdened with this desire because you have a story to tell.

So go write it. Then share it.

We want to read it.

And when you do publish it? Let me know, would you?

I can't wait to see what you do.

With all my heart, I say,

Onward!

ABOUT RACHAEL

Official Biography:

Rachael Herron is the bestselling author of the novels *The Ones Who Matter Most* (named a 2016 Editor's Pick by Library Journal), *Splinters of Light* and *Pack Up the Moon* (all from Penguin), the Darling Bay and the Cypress Hollow series, and the memoir, *A Life in Stitches* (Chronicle). She received her MFA in writing from Mills College, Oakland and she teaches writing in the extension programs at both UC Berkeley and Stanford. She's proud to be a New Zealander as well as a US citizen, though her Kiwi accent only comes out when she's very tired. She's honored to be a member of the NaNoWriMo Writers Board.

Coaching:

I offer 30-60 minute publishing consultations over Skype (this is the perfect time to run your outline by someone or to ask any questions that remain about memoir or any other part of the writing craft). You also get the mp3 of our talk, so you don't have to scribble notes till your hand cramps. See more at rachaelherron.com/coach.

Teaching

"**Rachael is one of the few speakers we've ever had at our conferences who has received a perfect score in one of our post-event surveys for her session.** In short, she resonates with our audience. And not just because she knows her stuff—she does—or because she's hilarious—she is—but because her honesty and earnestness come through in all her messaging."
Samantha Sanders, Writer's Digest

Bring me to your writer's group, your retreat, your Rotary club, whatever you'd like. I can teach this book in as little as two hours and up to a full-day (or two) course.
Email me for details. Rachael@rachaelherron.com

Memoir Prompts:

Would you like 365 days of memoir prompts sent to your inbox daily for just $25? Visit rachaelherron.com/memoir to grab some inspiration for the days you're running short.

Writer's Group

And do join my writer's email list! Every week, I send out an encouraging email, totally free, nudging you to *do the work* that matters most to you. You'll also have opportunities to join my review team and hear about my writing retreats before anyone else. But mostly, it's a free, weekly, very friendly ass-kicking. Go to rachaelherron.com/write to sign up.

And now, those two magic words, the same ones you're going for:

THE END

FOOTNOTES

1. Ben Yagoda, Memoir: A History (New York: Riverhead Books, 2009)

2. I'm frequently asked if I'd recommend going the MFA route. To be honest, I do not. I enjoyed my time at Mills College, and I abuse my alumna status terribly (as I write these words, I'm ensconced in a cozy carrel at the Mills Library, listening to students cough their way through studying for finals. It's quite cheerful. Out the window I watch bicyclists and dog walkers on the sidewalk. I take fashion notes from the nineteen-year-olds and spy on their current shoe trends). But my master's put me fifty-thousand dollars in debt, an amount hard to justify when I learned more by just writing and by joining professional writers' organizations than I ever did in the program. If you do want an MFA (it's useful for teaching, I'll grant you that), and you don't have to put yourself in debt to do it? Go for it. Don't strap more debt to yourself to get one, though. I did pay off my student loan with writing monies, but this is unfortunately not common.

3. Phillip Lopate, To Show and to Tell: The Craft of Literary Nonfiction (New York: Free Press, 2013), loc. 205-206, Kindle.

4. Mary Karr, The Art of Memoir (New York: HarperCollins, 2015), 29, Kindle.

5. Julian Barnes, Levels of Life (London: Vintage, 2013).

6. "Elizabeth hippocampal complex," Current Opinion in Neurobiology 14 (2004): 198-hippocampal complex," Current Opinion in Neurobiology 14 (2004): 198-202, http://www.psych.nyu.edu/phelpslab/papers/04_CON_V14.pdf.

7. Anne Lamott, Bird by Bird (New York: Anchor Books, 1995).

8. Meredith Maran, Why We Write About Ourselves (Penguin Publishing Group, 2016), 135.

9. Dani Shapiro, "Writing Memoir and Having Patience," How Do You Write (Podcast), Ep. 26, December 8, 2016, http://howdoyouwrite.libsyn.com/podcast/ep-026-dani-shapiro.

10. Mary Karr, The Art of Memoir (New York: HarperCollins, 2015), 119, Kindle.

11. Stephen S. Hall, "How We Might Take the Trauma out of Bad Memories," MIT Technology Review, May 11, 2017, https://www.technologyreview.com/s/515981/repairing-bad-memories/.

12. Mary Karr, The Art of Memoir (New York: HarperCollins, 2015), 11, Kindle.

13. Hilary Mantel, Giving Up the Ghost: A Memoir (New York: Picador, 2004), Locations 1406-1412, Kindle.

14. Phillip Lopate, To Show and to Tell: The Craft of Literary Nonfiction (New York: Free Press, 2013), loc. 228-231, Kindle.

15. Cal Newport, Deep Work: rules for focused success in a distracted world (New York: Hachette Book Group, 2016)

16. Jill Swenson, "The Many Subgenres of Memoir," Swenson Book Development, March 30, 2013, https://www.swensonbookdevelopment.com/blog/2013/the-many-subgenres-of-memoir/.

17. Larry Brooks, Story Engineering (Cincinnati, OH: Writers Digest Books, 2011), 151, Kindle.

18. Robbie Gonzalez, "Why Do We Work Better Under Pressure?" io9, April 11, 2014, http://io9.gizmodo.com/why-do-we-work-better-under-pressure-1553149028.

19. Keith Oatley, "Why Fiction May Be Twice as True as Fact: Fiction as Cognitive and Emotional Simulation," Review of General Psychology 3, No. 2, (1999): 101-117, http://faculty.weber.edu/eamsel/Research%20Groups/Fiction/Oatly%20(1999).pdf.

20. J. Gonzalez et al., "Reading cinnamon activates olfactory brain regions," Neuroimage 15, No. 32 (May 2, 2006): 906-12, https://www.ncbi.nlm.nih.gov/pubmed/16651007.

21. Brené Brown, "3 Things You Can Do to Stop a Shame Spiral," Oprah's Lifeclass, Oprah Winfrey Network, Oct 6, 2013, video, https://www.youtube.com/watch?v=TdtabNt4S7E

22. Brené Brown, The Gifts of Imperfection: Let Go of Who You Think You're Supposed to Be and Embrace Who You Are (Center City, MN: Hazelden, 2010).

23. Heidi Julavits, The Folded Clock: A Diary (New York: Knopf Doubleday Publishing Group, 2015), 125, Kindle.

24. Mary Karr, The Art of Memoir (New York: HarperCollins. 2015), Kindle.

25. Beth Kephart, "It Goes Like This: Writing Your Memoir," The Huffington Post, August 6, 2013, https://www.huffingtonpost.com/beth-kephart/it-goes-like-this-writing_b_3713553.html

26. Phillip Lopate, To Show and to Tell: The Craft of Literary Nonfiction (New York: Free Press, 2013), loc. 393-394, Kindle.

27. John Scalzi, "Writing: Find the Time or Don't," Whatever (blog), September 16, 2010, https://whatever.scalzi.com/2010/09/16/writing-find-the-time-or-dont/